Welcome to a journey through the most gripping, surprising, and downright bizarre tales from World War II. We wanted to bring you classic stories alongside some you may have never heard before, all filled with extraordinary characters and unbelievable events that shaped the world's most devastating conflict. From daring secret missions and unexpected heroes to quirky animal recruits and mind-boggling inventions, you'll discover the fascinating facets of the war that you won't find in your average history book.

Prepare to be amazed as we delve into the cunning strategies, brave individuals, and peculiar occurrences that played out on the global stage. Along the way, you'll also encounter some fun quizzes to test your memory and knowledge. Whether you're a history buff or a casual reader, these stories will captivate your imagination and provide a fresh perspective on the war. So sit back, turn the page, and embark on an unforgettable adventure through the lesser-known side of World War II.

We shall fight on the beaches, we shall fight on the landing grounds, we shall fight in the fields and in the streets, we shall fight in the hills; we shall never surrender." — Winston Churchill

"When you go home, tell them of us and say, for your tomorrow, we gave our today." — John Maxwell Edmonds

"He alone, who owns the youth, gains the future." — Adolf Hitler

"No man is entitled to the blessings of freedom unless he be vigilant in its preservation." — General Douglas MacArthur

Contents

Time-Ticking Tales: The Carpenter's Conspiracy to Kill Hitler	6
The Perfect Setting	6
Crafting the Bomb	7
Why It Failed	8
Escape from Germany	9
Who Am I – Easy	11
A Bear Named Wojtek	14
From Neutral Island to Strategic Stronghold: Iceland's WWII Transformation	16
Eva Braun's Icelandic Holiday	16
The United Kingdom's Invasion of Iceland	17
The Arrival of American Forces	18
Post-War Economic Boom	18
Other Occupations with Little or No Resistance	20
The Perils of the Sky: Pilot Training in WWII	23
Winston Churchill's Life Through His Quotes	26
Did you know?	29
Unstoppable Hiroo Onoda: The Soldier Who Fought On	30
Years of Survival	30
A Lone Soldier	31
The Discovery	31
The Reception	33
Controversy and Debate	33
Adjusting to a New Japan	34
Life After the War	34
Japanese Army & Soldiers Facts	35
What Battle Am I?	37
Gandhi's Message of Peace to Hitler	42
A Commander's Collapse: Himmler's Retreat to a Spa	44
Adolf Hitler's Life Through His Quotes	46

D-Day (Normandy Invasion) Fact File	49
Italian Fascism and Italy during WW2 Quiz	**51**
Ion Antonescu: The Tyrant of Romania	**55**
Brutal Policies and Massacres	55
Military Campaigns	57
Decline and Fall	58
Charles de Gaulle's Life Through His Quotes	**62**
The Nazi Party Quiz	**66**
Questions	66
Battle of Stalingrad	71
The Night Witches: Silent Shadows of the Eastern Front	**73**
Bat Bombs: America's Unconventional Weapon Experiment	75
Who Am I - Medium	**78**
Canine Warriors: The Tragic Tale of Soviet Anti-Tank Dogs	**81**
Joseph Stalin's Life Through His Quotes	**83**
Unlikely Allies: The Battle of Castle Itter	**87**
A Fierce Defense	88
Nuremberg Trials Fact File	90
Fire from the Sky: Japan's Failed Incendiary Balloon Campaign	**92**
The Fu-Go Balloons	92
The Code Talkers: Native American Linguists of World War II	**95**
Other Encryption Methods Used During World War II	97
Wartime Japan Quiz	**99**
Father of the Atomic Bomb	**103**
The Nazis' Sun Gun: A Sci-Fi Dream of Destruction	**106**
Other Inventions the Nazis Tried	107
Project Habakkuk: Britain's Icy Ambition	**108**
Engineering the Ice Carrier	108
Lady Death: The Fearsome Sniper of the Soviet Union	**111**
A Diplomatic Warrior	112
Pearl Harbor Attack	114
The Ghost Army: America's Masters of Deception	**116**
Ingenious Tactics	116
The Hidden Cave of Gibraltar: The Royal Navy's Secret	

Operations Centre 119
    Preparation and Execution 119
Operation Tannenbaum: Hitler's Unseen Plan to Invade Switzerland 122
    Switzerland's Defiance 123
Operation Unthinkable: Churchill's Secret War Plan 125
    The Plan's Objectives 125
    Secrecy and Sensitivity 126
Who Am I – Hard 128
Mad Jack Churchill: The Bagpipe-Playing, Sword-Wielding Soldier 131
Timeline of WW2 134
Cult of Hitler 138
    Early Life and Ideology Formation 138
    Mein Kampf and Ideological Blueprint 138
    Rise to Power 139
    The Cult of Hitler 139
Benito Mussolini's Life Through His Quotes 142
The Death of Mussolini: The Downfall of Italian Fascism .. 146
    The Fate of Mussolini's Brain 147
Best World War II Films 149
Propaganda 153
    Allied Enlistment 153
    Axis Enlistment 153
    Walt Disney's Role in War Support through Propaganda . 154
    Churchill's Dilemma 155

Time-Ticking Tales: The Carpenter's Conspiracy to Kill Hitler

Ever wonder how a humble carpenter almost changed the course of history with a ticking bomb and a brilliant plan? Well, fasten your seatbelts, because you're about to dive into the riveting story of Georg Elser, a man who dared to challenge one of the most infamous tyrants of all time. In this book, we uncover the wild and incredible tale of Elser's plot to assassinate Adolf Hitler, a plot that, had it succeeded, might have altered the fate of the world forever.

Meet **Georg Elser**, a quiet, unassuming carpenter from the picturesque Swabian Alps. Don't let his modest profession fool you – Georg was anything but ordinary. His meticulous nature, honed through years of woodworking, and his deep-seated opposition to the Nazi regime made him the perfect candidate for an audacious plan. Fueled by a desire to stop the spread of evil, Elser embarked on a daring mission to eliminate Hitler and save countless lives.

The Perfect Setting

In 1939, the **Bürgerbräukeller in Munich** was more than just a beer hall; it was a hallowed ground for the Nazi Party, steeped in the history and mythology of the regime. Every year, on November 8th, Adolf Hitler delivered a speech here to commemorate the failed Beer Hall Putsch of 1923, an event that had become a cornerstone of Nazi propaganda. The gathering was highly anticipated, drawing key figures of the Nazi hierarchy and numerous supporters. For Georg Elser, this event represented a unique and critical opportunity to strike at the heart of the Nazi leadership.

Recognizing the significance of the occasion, Elser began to plan meticulously. The annual commemoration provided a predictable setting, with Hitler's attendance almost guaranteed. This predictability allowed Elser to devise a detailed strategy, knowing exactly where and when Hitler would be. The Bürgerbräukeller, with its symbolic importance and the presence of high-ranking Nazis, was the perfect stage for his bold attempt to change the course of history. Elser's resolve was firm; he was determined to take this one chance to stop Hitler and his reign of terror.

Crafting the Bomb

Elser's workshop became the secret headquarters for his audacious plan. Amidst sawdust, tools, and the smell of wood, he worked late into the night, painstakingly crafting a bomb that was as sophisticated as it was deadly. This was no ordinary explosive device; it was a marvel of engineering, designed with a meticulous timing mechanism that would ensure detonation at the precise moment of Hitler's speech. Elser's background as a skilled carpenter and his innate ingenuity came together in this laborious task, reflecting his unwavering commitment to his mission.

The bomb's construction required incredible precision and patience. Elser's goal was not only to kill Hitler but to do so without causing unnecessary collateral damage. He carefully calculated the bomb's placement and timing to maximize its effectiveness while minimizing harm to others. This intricate work was a testament to Elser's dedication and technical skill, embodying his belief that even a single, well-planned action could make a profound difference. His determination and resourcefulness were the driving forces behind this extraordinary endeavor, highlighting his courage in the face of overwhelming danger.

Why It Failed

Despite all of Georg Elser's meticulous planning and careful execution, fate had a different outcome in store. The night of November 8, 1939, began as anticipated, with Hitler arriving at the Bürgerbräukeller and delivering his annual speech. However, an unexpected turn of events occurred: **Hitler decided to cut his speech short and leave the venue earlier than planned**. This change, prompted by worsening weather conditions that threatened his return flight to Berlin, caused him to depart the beer hall just minutes before Elser's bomb was set to detonate.

At precisely 9:20 PM, the bomb exploded with devastating force, reducing the pillar near the speaker's podium to rubble and causing significant destruction within the hall. The explosion killed eight people and injured sixty-two others, but Hitler was already safely on his way back to Berlin. The failure of the bomb to kill its intended target was a crushing blow to Elser, whose carefully laid plans had hinged on precise timing.

In the aftermath, the Nazi regime launched an extensive investigation to find the perpetrator of the bombing. Elser, attempting to flee to Switzerland, was apprehended by border guards. During his interrogation, he confessed to the plot, providing detailed accounts of his actions and motivations. Despite the compelling evidence he presented, many in the Nazi leadership initially believed that the British intelligence service was behind the assassination attempt, refusing to accept that a lone carpenter could orchestrate such a sophisticated plot.

Elser was subsequently transferred to various prisons and concentration camps, where he endured years of harsh imprisonment and interrogation. Despite the severity of his situation, he remained resolute, never wavering in his belief that his actions were justified and necessary. His failure to assassinate Hitler was not due to a lack of planning or courage but to the unpredictable nature of events beyond his control.

Escape from Germany

Following the failed assassination attempt, Elser knew he had to escape Germany to avoid certain execution. His plan was to cross the border into Switzerland, a neutral country where he believed he could find refuge. On the night of the bombing, Elser made his way to the Swiss border, hoping to evade the tightening net of the Nazi authorities who were hunting for the bomber.

However, Elser's escape attempt was fraught with challenges. As he approached the border, he was detained by suspicious border guards who found incriminating evidence on him, including wire cutters and sketches of the Bürgerbräukeller bomb. These discoveries led to his immediate arrest and subsequent transfer to German authorities. Despite his attempts to explain his actions, the guards remained unconvinced and handed him over for further interrogation.

During his interrogation, Elser's captors were initially skeptical of his lone wolf narrative, suspecting a larger conspiracy at play. Elser, however, consistently maintained that he had acted alone, driven by his deep-seated opposition to the Nazi regime. Despite his clear and detailed confession, the Nazi leadership struggled to believe that a single individual could have orchestrated such a complex and audacious plot without external assistance.

Ultimately, Elser's failure to escape Germany sealed his fate. He was held as a high-profile prisoner, subjected to brutal interrogation methods, and transferred between various concentration camps. His capture and subsequent imprisonment highlighted the risks and challenges faced by those who dared to resist the Nazi regime, serving as a sobering reminder of the high stakes involved in such acts of defiance.

P.S. Personally, I think Georg Elser is a hero who faced unfortunate circumstances. Imagine if there hadn't been bad weather that night – history might have taken a very different turn. But did you know there were actually many failed plots to kill Hitler? Here are a few:

- **Operation Valkyrie (July 20, 1944)**: A bomb planted by Colonel Claus von Stauffenberg in Hitler's Wolf's Lair headquarters. The explosion killed four people, but Hitler survived.
- **The Beer Hall Putsch (November 8-9, 1923)**: Hitler's early failed coup attempt, which resulted in a brief imprisonment but ultimately propelled him to prominence.
- **The Oster Conspiracy (1938)**: Planned by German General Hans Oster and other high-ranking officers to overthrow Hitler during the Sudeten Crisis. It never materialized due to the Munich Agreement.
- **Operation Foxley (1944)**: A British SOE plan to assassinate Hitler at his Berghof residence, involving snipers and explosives. The mission was never executed.
- **The Elser Bomb Plot (November 8, 1939)**: The subject of this story, Elser's attempt involved a time-bomb at the Bürgerbräukeller. Hitler left early, narrowly escaping death.
- **The Tresckow Plot (March 13, 1943)**: Major General Henning von Tresckow placed a bomb on Hitler's plane. The bomb failed to detonate due to a faulty fuse.

Did You Know?

Adolf Hitler had a paranoia that would make any foodie cringe! Terrified of being poisoned, Hitler employed a team of fifteen food tasters to sample every meal before it touched his lips. Imagine the culinary suspense: each dish, a potential plot twist in a high-stakes drama of espionage and gastronomy! His head taster, Margot Woelk, later revealed that the team had to taste every bite of his strictly vegetarian meals, living in constant fear of a fatal flavor. It's a reminder that even dictators have their own quirky, albeit sinister, fears!

Who Am I – Easy

1. I was the Prime Minister of the United Kingdom during most of World War II. Known for my rousing speeches and steadfast leadership, I played a crucial role in leading the Allies to victory against the Axis powers. My famous speeches included the "We shall fight on the beaches" address.
   Who am I?

   _____

2. I was a German-born physicist who fled to the United States before World War II. My famous letter to President Franklin D. Roosevelt helped initiate the Manhattan Project, which developed the atomic bomb. Despite my contributions, I advocated for peace and disarmament after the war.
   Who am I?

   _____

3. I was the Supreme Commander of the Allied Expeditionary Force in Europe and later became the 34th President of the United States. I led the successful invasion of Normandy on D-Day, which was a turning point in the war against Nazi Germany.
   Who am I?

   _____

4. I was a French general and statesman who led the Free French Forces during World War II. After the liberation of France, I became the head of the Provisional Government and later founded the Fifth Republic, serving as its first President.
   Who am I?

5. I was a Soviet military commander known for my pivotal role in the Battle of Stalingrad, one of the deadliest battles in history. My leadership helped turn the tide against the Nazis on the Eastern Front, leading to the eventual defeat of Germany.
Who am I?

Answers

1. **Winston Churchill**, born in 1874, served as the Prime Minister of the United Kingdom during most of World War II. His leadership and stirring speeches, including the famous "We shall fight on the beaches" address, inspired the British people to stand firm against the Axis powers. Churchill's determination and ability to rally the Allies were instrumental in achieving victory. He remains a symbol of resilience and defiance in the face of adversity.

2. **Albert Einstein**, born in 1879 in Ulm, Germany, was a brilliant physicist who fled to the United States to escape the Nazi regime. His famous letter to President Franklin D. Roosevelt, written in 1939, warned of the potential for Nazi

Germany to develop atomic weapons and urged the U.S. to begin similar research, leading to the Manhattan Project. Einstein's later years were marked by his advocacy for peace and nuclear disarmament, reflecting his deep commitment to humanitarian causes.

3. **Dwight D. Eisenhower** Born in 1890 in Denison, Texas, was the Supreme Commander of the Allied Expeditionary Force in Europe during World War II. He planned and executed the D-Day invasion on June 6, 1944, which marked a critical turning point in the war. After the war, Eisenhower's leadership qualities and military success propelled him to become the 34th President of the United States, serving two terms from 1953 to 1961.

4. **Charles de Gaulle**, born in 1890 in Lille, France, was a French general and statesman who led the Free French Forces against Nazi Germany during World War II. After the liberation of France, de Gaulle headed the Provisional Government and worked to restore democracy. In 1958, he founded the Fifth Republic and became its first President, shaping modern France's political landscape. De Gaulle's legacy as a symbol of French resistance and his vision for France endure in history.

5. **Georgy Zhukov,** born in 1896 in Strelkovka, Russia, was a prominent Soviet military commander whose leadership was crucial in several key battles during World War II. Most notably, he orchestrated the defense and eventual counterattack at the Battle of Stalingrad, which turned the tide against the Nazis on the Eastern Front. Zhukov's strategic brilliance and determination contributed significantly to the ultimate defeat of Nazi Germany. He is celebrated as one of the greatest military commanders in history.

A Bear Named Wojtek

During World War II, the Polish Army had an extraordinary and unique recruit: a bear named Wojtek. Yes, you read that right—a bear! Wojtek, a Syrian brown bear, joined the ranks of the Polish II Corps and quickly became much more than just a mascot.

Wojtek's journey began in 1942 in Iran. Discovered as a tiny cub by Polish soldiers, he was bought from a young boy and adopted into the unit. The soldiers raised him, and Wojtek soon became one of the gang. This bear didn't just sit around; he actively participated in their daily routines, even picking up some amusing habits like drinking beer, munching on cigarettes, and engaging in playful wrestling matches with his human comrades.

But Wojtek wasn't just there for the fun. His most famous moment came during the Battle of Monte Cassino in Italy in 1944. Wojtek helped transport heavy crates of ammunition, often carrying boxes that typically required four men to lift. Picture this bear standing on his hind legs, dutifully hauling shells as if he were just another soldier—which, technically, he was! To ensure he could travel with them, the army enlisted Wojtek as a private and later promoted him to corporal for his services.

Wojtek became a symbol of the Polish II Corps, with his image carrying an artillery shell adopted as the official emblem of the 22nd Transport Company. After the war, Wojtek retired to the Edinburgh Zoo in Scotland, where he lived out his days, continuing to charm visitors with his incredible story.

- Wojtek's legacy lives on in books, documentaries, and statues, serving as a heartwarming reminder of the unbreakable bond between soldiers and their animal companions. His story is not just a quirky footnote in history; it's a testament to resilience, camaraderie, and the extraordinary lengths to which friendship can go—even in the midst of war.

- **Pigeons (Allied Forces):** Employed by the U.S. Army Signal Corps and the British Army for delivering messages. Pigeons carried vital communications across enemy lines when other methods failed, with some being awarded medals for their service.

- **Dogs (U.S. Army):** Used for sentry duty, message delivery, and mine detection. The U.S. Army trained dogs to perform various tasks, including scouting and tracking. Notably, some dogs were awarded medals for bravery in combat.

- **Horses (German Army):** Relied upon heavily for transportation and carrying supplies, especially on the Eastern Front where mechanized transport was limited. Horses were essential for moving artillery and other heavy equipment in rough terrain.

- **Mules (Allied Forces in Burma):** Used by British and Indian troops in the Burma Campaign for transporting supplies through the dense jungles and mountainous regions. Mules were critical in ensuring that troops received necessary provisions in otherwise inaccessible areas.

- **Cats (British Royal Navy):** Served on naval vessels to control the rodent population and boost crew morale. Cats aboard ships such as the HMS Amethyst played a vital role in maintaining hygiene and preventing disease by keeping the ship free of rats.

From Neutral Island to Strategic Stronghold: Iceland's WWII Transformation

One lesser-known aspect of Adolf Hitler's life is his fascination with Iceland, a country he admired for its Aryan heritage and remote location. Hitler believed that Iceland embodied the purest form of the Aryan race due to its relative isolation and lack of genetic mixing with other populations. This admiration extended to his inner circle, including his wife, Eva Braun.

Eva Braun's Icelandic Holiday

In the late 1930s, Eva Braun, Hitler's long-time companion and later his wife, took a clandestine holiday to Iceland. The trip was intended as both a respite from the intense political atmosphere in Germany and an opportunity to explore a land that Hitler had often spoken about with great interest. Iceland's pristine landscapes and sparsely populated regions offered a stark contrast to the increasingly militarized Germany.

- **Secrecy and Security:** Eva Braun's Icelandic holiday was shrouded in secrecy, with only a few close associates aware of her travels to ensure her safety and maintain Hitler's strict control over his inner circle's movements.
- **Natural Beauty and Solitude:** During her visit, Braun marveled at Iceland's untouched natural landscapes, enjoying the solitude and serenity that the remote island offered, a stark contrast to the escalating tensions in Germany.

- **Cultural Exploration:** While in Iceland, Braun took the opportunity to immerse herself in local culture, visiting traditional Icelandic villages and learning about the country's unique history and folklore.

At the beginning of World War II, Iceland was part of the Kingdom of Denmark. Denmark's control over Iceland had been mostly nominal, and Iceland had its own parliament and government. When Germany invaded Denmark on April 9, 1940, Iceland declared itself neutral and aimed to stay out of the conflict. However, Iceland's strategic location in the North Atlantic soon drew the attention of both Allied and Axis powers.

The United Kingdom's Invasion of Iceland

On May 10, 1940, British forces invaded Iceland in a mission codenamed "Operation Fork." The British government feared that Germany might invade Iceland and use it as a base to control the North Atlantic, which would threaten the vital supply lines between North America and Europe. The Icelandic government protested the invasion but did not resist militarily, as Iceland had no standing army.

The British occupation brought significant changes to Iceland. Thousands of British troops were stationed on the island, leading to a rapid construction of airfields, harbors, and other military infrastructure. This influx of foreign soldiers and the subsequent economic activity disrupted Iceland's traditional, relatively insular way of life. While the occupation provided an economic boost, it also led to social tensions and cultural clashes.

Iceland's strategic importance lay in its position along the North Atlantic shipping lanes. Control of Iceland allowed the Allies to protect convoys carrying vital supplies from North America to the United Kingdom and the Soviet Union. The airfields and naval bases established in Iceland enabled the Allies to conduct anti-submarine patrols and provide air cover for the convoys, significantly reducing the threat posed by German U-boats.

The Arrival of American Forces

In 1941, the United States, although not yet officially at war, took over the defense of Iceland from the British under an agreement with the Icelandic government. This move was part of the broader Lend-Lease Act and was aimed at bolstering the defense of the North Atlantic. American troops began arriving in July 1941, and Iceland became a crucial link in the transatlantic defense network.

The presence of British and American troops brought a mixture of benefits and challenges to Iceland. On one hand, the construction projects and military spending boosted the local economy, creating jobs and improving infrastructure. On the other hand, the cultural and social impact of thousands of foreign soldiers strained Icelandic society. Issues such as increased crime, changes in social norms, and the impact on Icelandic women were notable.

Throughout the war, Iceland played a critical role in the Battle of the Atlantic. The bases on the island allowed Allied forces to extend their reach, protecting convoys and launching anti-submarine operations. The airfields were used for long-range patrols that significantly reduced the effectiveness of the German U-boat campaigns, thus safeguarding the vital supply lines necessary for the Allied war effort.

Post-War Economic Boom

The end of World War II brought significant changes to Iceland. The infrastructure developed during the war laid the foundation for post-war economic growth. The airfields and ports built by the Allies became crucial components of Iceland's transport and fishing industries. The war years had also introduced Icelanders to new technologies and practices that would continue to benefit the nation.

In 1944, while still under Allied occupation, Iceland took a significant step towards full sovereignty. On June 17, 1944, Iceland declared itself a republic, formally ending its union with Denmark. This move was overwhelmingly supported by the Icelandic people and was a direct result of the changing political landscape brought about by the war.

During the Cold War, Iceland's strategic importance did not diminish. The United States maintained a military presence on the island as part of NATO's defensive strategy against the Soviet Union. The Keflavik Air Base, established during the war, became a key point for monitoring Soviet submarine activity in the North Atlantic.

The Allied occupation had lasting social and cultural impacts on Iceland. The exposure to foreign cultures and technologies during the war years accelerated modernization in Icelandic society. English began to be widely spoken, and American cultural influences became more prevalent. These changes were both welcomed and resisted by different segments of the population.

The economic boost from the war years and the subsequent American presence helped Iceland diversify its economy. The fishing industry remained a cornerstone, but the infrastructure improvements allowed for expansion into other sectors, such as tourism and aviation. The knowledge and skills gained during this period positioned Iceland for rapid post-war development.

Post-war relations with the United Kingdom were complex. While the British invasion had been a violation of Iceland's neutrality, the collaboration during the war and the economic benefits softened the long-term impact. The two countries maintained strong diplomatic and trade relationships, and the shared history of the war years became a point of mutual understanding.

The legacy of the Allied occupation is a mixed one. While it brought significant economic and infrastructural benefits, it also led to social disruptions and a loss of innocence for many Icelanders. The occupation period is remembered as a time of profound change that accelerated Iceland's transition into a modern nation.

The experiences of World War II and the subsequent American influence played a crucial role in shaping modern Icelandic identity. The rapid modernization and exposure to global cultures during the occupation years contributed to a more cosmopolitan outlook among Icelanders, while also strengthening national pride and the desire for independence.

The economic foundations laid during the war years set the stage for Iceland's post-war prosperity. Investments in infrastructure, education, and industry during the occupation period paid off, leading to sustained economic growth and an improved standard of living for Icelanders in the decades following the war.

Today, Iceland continues to hold strategic importance in the North Atlantic. The legacy of the wartime and Cold War years has ensured that Iceland remains a key player in regional security. The country's modern military agreements and its role in international organizations like NATO are a testament to its ongoing strategic significance.

Other Occupations with Little or No Resistance

- **Germany's Anschluss of Austria (1938):** Austria was annexed into Nazi Germany with little opposition, as many Austrians welcomed the unification. The move was portrayed as a restoration of German-Austrian unity, and the Nazi regime used propaganda to showcase the event as a peaceful and joyous reunion. The Austrian government was pressured into capitulation, and the Anschluss was formalized without significant conflict.
- **Annexation of the Baltic States by the Soviet Union (1940):** Estonia, Latvia, and Lithuania were occupied and annexed by the Soviet Union with minimal resistance. The

Soviet Union had signed mutual assistance treaties with these countries, which allowed for the stationing of Soviet troops. Under threat of invasion, the Baltic governments accepted Soviet demands, leading to the establishment of pro-Soviet regimes and subsequent annexation.

- **Invasion of Czechoslovakia (1939):** After the Munich Agreement in 1938, which allowed Germany to annex the Sudetenland, Germany occupied the rest of Czechoslovakia in March 1939 with little military resistance. The Czech government capitulated without a fight, leading to the dissolution of Czechoslovakia and the establishment of the Protectorate of Bohemia and Moravia under German control.
- **Occupation of Denmark (1940):** Germany invaded Denmark on April 9, 1940, during World War II, and the Danish government quickly surrendered. The invasion was swift, and the Danish government chose to cooperate with the Germans to avoid unnecessary destruction and loss of life. Denmark remained under German occupation until 1945.
- **Occupation of Norway (1940):** While Norway did offer some resistance, the country was quickly occupied by Germany. The invasion began on April 9, 1940, and by June, Norwegian forces had surrendered. The strategic importance of Norway's ports and coastline made it a target for German occupation.
- **Occupation of Manchuria by Japan (1931):** Japan invaded and occupied Manchuria with little effective Chinese resistance. The Mukden Incident, a staged event by Japanese military personnel, provided a pretext for the invasion. By 1932, Japan had established the puppet state of Manchukuo, which remained under Japanese control until the end of World War II.
- **Occupation of Albania by Italy (1939):** Italy invaded and occupied Albania on April 7, 1939, facing little resistance from Albanian forces. King Zog of Albania fled into exile,

and Albania was incorporated into the Italian Empire. The occupation was part of Mussolini's ambition to expand Italian influence in the Balkans.
- **Invasion of Tibet by China (1950):** China invaded Tibet and quickly established control over the region with limited resistance. The People's Liberation Army entered Tibet in October 1950, and by 1951, Tibet had signed the Seventeen Point Agreement, recognizing Chinese sovereignty. The invasion led to significant changes in Tibetan society and governance.
- **Invasion of Kuwait by Iraq (1990):** Iraq invaded Kuwait on August 2, 1990, with little military opposition. The swift occupation was part of Saddam Hussein's plan to annex Kuwait and gain control of its vast oil reserves. The invasion led to international condemnation and the subsequent Gulf War, where a coalition led by the United States liberated Kuwait in 1991.

The Perils of the Sky: Pilot Training in WWII

World War II marked a significant turning point in military history, as it was one of the first major conflicts to extensively incorporate aviation. This new dimension of warfare necessitated a massive rush to train thousands of new pilots, many of whom were young and inexperienced. However, the urgency to get pilots into the air often meant that the aviation training programs were hastily assembled, with insufficient safety measures and incomplete protocols.

The consequences of this rushed training were dire. Over 15,000 deaths occurred during pilot training alone, a staggering number that highlights the dangerous conditions under which these young aviators were learning to fly. These fatalities were primarily due to pilot error and mechanical failures, as the new recruits struggled to master the complex machinery of their aircraft with minimal instruction and practice.

One of the most notorious aircraft of the time was the B-24 Liberator bomber, which quickly earned the grim nickname 'the flying coffin.' The B-24's reputation stemmed from its high accident rate, both during training and in combat. Its design, which prioritized payload capacity and range over ease of handling, made it particularly challenging for inexperienced pilots. As a result, many trainees lost their lives in accidents involving this plane.

The scale of these training fatalities is sobering. To put it into perspective, around 52,000 American flight crew members died during World War II. Of these, nearly 30%—about 15,000—died outside of combat, primarily during training exercises. This statistic underscores the inherent dangers of pilot training at the time and the steep learning curve faced by those who aspired to take to the skies.

The high rate of training accidents was a significant concern for military leaders. Efforts were made to improve training protocols and aircraft safety, but the rapid pace of the war often meant that these measures were too little, too late for many. The necessity to produce combat-ready pilots quickly often overshadowed the need for thorough and safe training programs.

Despite these challenges, many pilots emerged from training to become skilled aviators who played crucial roles in the war effort. Their perseverance and bravery in the face of such high risks are testaments to their dedication and resolve. The survivors of these perilous training programs went on to engage in critical missions that helped shape the outcome of the war.

The legacy of these training fatalities serves as a poignant reminder of the hidden costs of war. While much attention is given to the valor and sacrifice of those who died in combat, it is equally important to remember those who lost their lives preparing to serve. Their contributions, though less celebrated, were essential to the war effort and deserve recognition.

In hindsight, the lessons learned from these tragedies have helped shape modern aviation training programs. Today, the emphasis on safety and thorough instruction ensures that new pilots are better prepared and protected. The sacrifices of those who trained under such perilous conditions during World War II have ultimately contributed to safer skies for future generations of aviators.

- During World War II, the United States established the Women Airforce Service Pilots (WASP) program to address the shortage of male pilots. These female pilots were trained to fly non-combat missions, such as ferrying aircraft, towing targets for live anti-aircraft gun practice, and transporting cargo. Despite facing gender discrimination and not being granted military status during the war, the WASPs played a crucial role in the war effort and proved that women could handle the rigors of military aviation.

- The Allied invasion of Normandy, known as D-Day or Operation Overlord, involved a massive airborne component, with thousands of paratroopers and glider-borne troops being deployed behind enemy lines. During this operation, numerous pilots faced significant risks. Many were shot down by anti-aircraft fire or crashed due to poor weather conditions and navigational challenges. The bravery and sacrifices of these pilots were instrumental in the success of the invasion, which was a turning point in the war.

Winston Churchill's Life Through His Quotes

"I am prepared to meet my Maker. Whether my Maker is prepared for the great ordeal of meeting me is another matter."

This quote reflects Churchill's characteristic wit and his belief in destiny and divine providence. Born on November 30, 1874, into an aristocratic family, Churchill's early life was marked by a strong sense of purpose and ambition. He pursued a military career, serving in Cuba, India, Sudan, and South Africa. His boldness and self-confidence were evident from a young age, setting the stage for his later roles in British politics and leadership.

"We make a living by what we get, but we make a life by what we give."

Churchill's commitment to public service and his belief in contributing to society is encapsulated in this quote. Elected to Parliament in 1900, he held various key positions, including First Lord of the Admiralty during World War I. His advocacy for social reforms, such as unemployment insurance and workers' rights, demonstrated his dedication to improving the lives of ordinary people, shaping his legacy as a statesman who valued giving back to society.

"Never give in—never, never, never, never, in nothing great or small, large or petty—never give in except to

convictions of honour and good sense."

This quote epitomizes Churchill's indomitable spirit and perseverance. His career was marked by numerous setbacks, including political defeats and controversies. Despite these challenges, Churchill's resilience was unwavering, most notably during the "wilderness years" of the 1930s when he warned against the rise of Nazi Germany while being out of favor politically. His steadfastness in the face of adversity became a defining trait of his leadership.

"Success is not final, failure is not fatal: it is the courage to continue that counts."

Churchill's pragmatic view of success and failure is highlighted in this quote. His leadership during World War II exemplified this philosophy. After becoming Prime Minister in 1940, he faced the monumental task of rallying Britain against the Axis powers. Despite early military setbacks, Churchill's courage and determination were crucial in sustaining British morale and resistance during the darkest days of the war, particularly during the Battle of Britain.

"I have nothing to offer but blood, toil, tears, and sweat."

This quote, from Churchill's first speech as Prime Minister in 1940, encapsulated his forthrightness and determination. It signaled his commitment to leading Britain through the existential threat posed by Nazi Germany. Churchill's ability to communicate the gravity of the situation, while simultaneously inspiring resolve and courage, was a key aspect of his leadership, earning him widespread respect and support.

> *"To each, there comes in their lifetime a special moment when they are figuratively tapped on the shoulder and offered the chance to do a very special thing, unique to them and fitted to their talents."*

Churchill believed in seizing opportunities and rising to challenges, as reflected in this quote. His decision to return to the Admiralty in 1939, just before the outbreak of World War II, and later his appointment as Prime Minister, were pivotal moments where his leadership and talents were uniquely suited to the needs of the nation. His strategic foresight and oratory skills were instrumental in guiding Britain through the war.

> *"You have enemies? Good. That means you've stood up for something, sometime in your life."*

Churchill's willingness to confront difficult issues and stand up for his beliefs often made him a polarizing figure. His staunch opposition to appeasement policies towards Nazi Germany and his advocacy for rearmament were initially unpopular but proved prescient. Churchill's ability to stand firm in his convictions, despite criticism and opposition, underscored his leadership style and his commitment to his principles.

> *"If you're going through hell, keep going."*

This quote reflects Churchill's philosophy of perseverance during the most challenging times. His leadership during the Blitz, when London and other cities were subjected to relentless bombing by the Luftwaffe, exemplified this tenacity. Churchill's resolve and his ability to inspire resilience in the British people were crucial in maintaining national morale and determination to continue fighting against the odds.

"The empires of the future are the empires of the mind."

Churchill's foresight and vision for the future are encapsulated in this quote. After World War II, he recognized the changing geopolitical landscape and the importance of intellectual and scientific advancement. His advocacy for European unity and his famous "Iron Curtain" speech highlighted his understanding of the emerging Cold War dynamics and the need for strategic alliances and cooperation. "

History will be kind to me, for I intend to write it."

Churchill's awareness of his historical legacy is evident in this quote. An accomplished writer and historian, he authored numerous works, including a six-volume history of World War II, which earned him the Nobel Prize in Literature in 1953. His writings not only documented his experiences and perspectives but also shaped the narrative of 20th-century history, ensuring his enduring influence and legacy.

Did you know?

Before his political career, Winston Churchill gained fame as a war correspondent, covering conflicts like the Cuban War of Independence, the Second Boer War, and the Mahdist War in Sudan. His daring escape from Boer captivity in 1899 made international headlines and bolstered his reputation, setting the stage for his future political success.

Unstoppable Hiroo Onoda: The Soldier Who Fought On

Ever heard of a soldier who refused to believe World War II had ended and continued his mission for nearly three decades? Meet Hiroo Onoda, a Japanese Imperial Army intelligence officer who remained loyal to his duties long after the war was over. In this book, we explore the incredible and bewildering story of Onoda, a man who lived in the jungles of the Philippines, fighting a war that had ended for everyone but him.

In December 1944, **Hiroo Onoda** was dispatched to the remote Philippine island of Lubang. His orders were clear: disrupt enemy activities and resist surrender at all costs. As Allied forces advanced, Onoda and a few comrades retreated deeper into the jungle. Unbeknownst to them, Japan would surrender in August 1945, but for Onoda, the war was far from over.

Years of Survival

For Hiroo Onoda, the dense jungles of Lubang became his battlefield and sanctuary. Along with a handful of comrades, he continued to wage a guerrilla war against the perceived enemy. Their existence was one of constant vigilance, surviving on what the jungle provided and engaging in sporadic skirmishes with local authorities and villagers. They avoided detection through their military training, becoming adept at jungle survival. Foraging for food, hunting wildlife, and raiding local farms became their means of subsistence.

Despite numerous efforts to inform them that the war had ended, Onoda and his men dismissed these as enemy propaganda. Leaflets dropped from the sky, radio broadcasts, and even messages from loudspeakers were all regarded with suspicion. The psychological toll of constant alertness and isolation was immense, yet Onoda's unwavering belief in his mission kept him and his men committed. Over the years, as his comrades either surrendered or were killed, Onoda's resolve never faltered, and he continued his solitary campaign.

A Lone Soldier

By 1950, Onoda was the only one left, his comrades having either died or surrendered. Alone but undeterred, he continued to live by the code of a soldier. His solitary existence in the jungle became legendary among the locals, who occasionally encountered this ghostly figure still clinging to the belief that Japan had not surrendered. Onoda's actions ranged from raiding villages for supplies to engaging in skirmishes with search parties sent to find him. His deep-seated commitment to his mission was both his strength and his curse.

The villagers grew accustomed to his presence, yet efforts to capture him were fraught with difficulty. Onoda's skills in evasion and survival made him an elusive target. Even as the years passed and the world moved on, Onoda remained stuck in time, bound by his orders and honor. His persistence became a symbol of both incredible loyalty and the tragic consequences of unwavering duty in the face of changing realities.

The Discovery

In 1974, nearly thirty years after World War II had ended, a young and eccentric Japanese adventurer named Norio Suzuki embarked on an incredible quest. Suzuki was not your average explorer; he was on a mission to find three elusive beings: Hiroo Onoda, the legendary soldier who refused to believe the war was over; a panda in the wild; and the mythical creature known as Bigfoot. With a heart full of curiosity and a taste for the extraordinary, Suzuki set off for the Philippines, determined to locate the enigmatic Onoda.

Suzuki's journey was anything but ordinary. Armed with little more than a backpack, a map, and his unwavering determination, he ventured into the dense jungles of Lubang Island. Suzuki's friends thought he was crazy, and perhaps he was – but his quirky ambition and adventurous spirit were exactly what the situation called for. Against all odds, Suzuki succeeded where countless search parties and well-meaning villagers had failed. He penetrated the jungle's depths, navigating its dangers with an almost magical intuition.

When Suzuki finally found Onoda, the scene was surreal. Imagine the moment: a battle-hardened soldier, still in uniform, emerging from the shadows of the jungle to meet a young, wide-eyed adventurer. Onoda, ever the skeptic, was cautious. Suzuki's initial attempts to convince him that the war had ended were met with suspicion. After all, Onoda had spent nearly three decades dismissing similar claims as enemy propaganda. But Suzuki's genuine persistence and infectious enthusiasm began to chip away at Onoda's defenses.

Suzuki wasn't just an adventurer; he was a bridge between two worlds. His warm personality and unwavering belief in his mission started to break through Onoda's hardened exterior. Suzuki's determination was not just to find Onoda but to understand him, to listen to his story, and to earn his trust. This personal connection proved crucial. Onoda, moved by Suzuki's sincerity, agreed to consider the possibility that the war might indeed be over – but only if he received confirmation from his former commanding officer.

This breakthrough moment was the beginning of the end of Onoda's incredible and tragic story of survival. Suzuki returned to Japan with tangible proof of his encounter, sparking a media frenzy and a concerted effort to bring Onoda back home. The Japanese government, recognizing the significance of this discovery, tracked down Major Yoshimi Taniguchi, Onoda's former superior. Taniguchi, now living a peaceful civilian life, was astonished to learn that one of his men was still holding out in the jungles of the Philippines.

On March 9, 1974, Major Taniguchi traveled to Lubang to personally deliver the orders that Onoda had awaited for nearly thirty years. In a solemn ceremony deep in the jungle, Taniguchi formally relieved Onoda of his duties. Dressed in his tattered uniform, Onoda saluted and handed over his sword, finally accepting that his war had ended. The surreal encounter between the dedicated soldier and his long-forgotten commander marked the end of one of history's most remarkable episodes of loyalty and perseverance.

The Reception

Upon his return to Japan, Hiroo Onoda received a hero's welcome. The media was abuzz with the astonishing tale of the soldier who had held out in the Philippine jungle for nearly thirty years. Crowds gathered to catch a glimpse of him, and he was showered with accolades and praise for his unwavering loyalty and dedication. His story captivated the nation, serving as a reminder of the extreme lengths to which individuals would go to fulfill their sense of duty.

However, Onoda's reception was not without controversy. The younger generation, born after the war, viewed his actions with a mix of admiration and bewilderment. They respected his perseverance but struggled to understand his prolonged resistance and the deaths that resulted from his raids on local villagers. The older generation, who had lived through the war, were more sympathetic to his plight, seeing him as a symbol of the sacrifices made by soldiers in the name of duty.

Controversy and Debate

Onoda's actions during his nearly three decades in hiding led to the deaths of several Filipino villagers and clashes with local authorities. This sparked a heated debate about the morality of his mission. Some saw him as a tragic figure caught in the grip of an outdated sense of honor, while others viewed him as a misguided soldier whose actions, though rooted in loyalty, caused unnecessary suffering.

The controversy also highlighted the rigorous training and indoctrination Japanese soldiers received during World War II. Onoda's persistence was a product of a military culture that emphasized absolute obedience and an unwavering commitment to one's orders. His story served as a poignant reminder of the psychological impact of such training and the human cost of war.

Adjusting to a New Japan

Reintegrating into post-war Japanese society was a profound challenge for Onoda. The Japan he returned to in 1974 was vastly different from the one he had left. It was now a democratic nation, aligned with Western powers and one of the most technologically advanced countries in the world. Onoda struggled to reconcile his wartime experiences with the modern, peaceful society he found himself in.

Onoda's reflections on contemporary Japan were mixed. He admired the nation's economic progress and technological advancements but lamented the loss of traditional values and the sense of honor that had once been so integral to Japanese identity. His story prompted many to reflect on how they would react if they had been isolated for thirty years, only to emerge into a world transformed by peace and progress.

Life After the War

After his return, Onoda penned a memoir detailing his extraordinary experiences, which became a bestseller in Japan. He also moved to Brazil for a time, where he ran a cattle ranch and sought solace away from the media spotlight. Onoda later returned to Japan and dedicated himself to youth education, founding a nature school to teach survival skills and instill a sense of discipline and respect for nature in young people.

Hiroo Onoda lived a long life, passing away on January 16, 2014, at the age of 91. His story remains one of the most compelling and debated episodes of World War II history, a testament to the extremes of human endurance and the complex nature of duty and loyalty.

P.S. Personally, I find Hiroo Onoda's story both fascinating and poignant. Imagine living in isolation for nearly three decades, convinced you were still at war! But did you know there are other mind-boggling tales from Japanese soldiers during World War II?

Over 3,800 Japanese pilots conducted suicide missions to crash their planes into enemy ships. These "divine wind" missions were a desperate tactic employed in the latter stages of the war, intended to inflict maximum damage on the Allied naval forces at the cost of the pilot's life.

Japanese Army & Soldiers Facts

- Japanese soldiers volunteered to pilot manned torpedoes on suicide missions to sink Allied ships. These Kaiten were essentially underwater kamikazes, designed to be steered directly into enemy vessels, sacrificing their operators in the process.
- Japanese soldiers frequently launched all-out, suicidal infantry charges known as "Banzai attacks" against enemy positions. These frenzied assaults were intended to overwhelm enemy defenses through sheer ferocity and numbers, often resulting in heavy Japanese casualties.
- Some Japanese soldiers survived for years in the jungles of Pacific islands, unaware the war had ended. Cut off from communication, they continued their guerrilla warfare, scavenging for food and living in isolation, convinced that their duty was still ongoing.
- Unit 731 conducted horrific biological and chemical warfare experiments on prisoners of war and civilians. This covert unit carried out some of the most inhumane experiments in history, including the testing of plague, anthrax, and other pathogens on live subjects.
- A plan to release plague-infected fleas over Southern California using kamikaze submarines was never executed. This chilling operation, known as Operation Cherry

Blossoms at Night, aimed to cause widespread panic and disease in the United States but was abandoned as Japan's situation became increasingly desperate.
- Japanese soldiers could convert their standard rifles into grenade launchers using specially designed grenades. This adaptation allowed infantry to deliver explosive ordnance at a greater range than hand-thrown grenades, enhancing their tactical flexibility in combat.
- Japanese soldiers were extensively trained for night combat, often launching surprise night attacks. This emphasis on nocturnal warfare aimed to exploit the cover of darkness, catching the enemy off guard and creating confusion within their ranks.
- Japan launched over 9,000 incendiary balloon bombs aimed at the U.S., with a few causing minor damage and casualties. These balloons, carried by the jet stream, were an early form of intercontinental warfare designed to start forest fires and create panic.

Did You Know?

When it comes to teaching World War II, Germany and Japan have distinct approaches shaped by their unique historical experiences. In Germany, education about the war is comprehensive and deeply introspective. The curriculum includes extensive coverage of the Holocaust, Nazi atrocities, and the war's devastating impact on Europe. German schools emphasize the importance of remembering these events to ensure they are never repeated, fostering a culture of reflection and responsibility.

In contrast, Japan's approach to teaching World War II often focuses more on the suffering experienced by Japanese civilians, particularly during events like the bombings of Hiroshima and Nagasaki. While the curriculum does cover Japan's militaristic actions and the war in the Pacific, there is generally less emphasis on wartime atrocities committed by Japanese forces. This difference in focus can lead to varied perceptions and understandings of the war among students in each country, reflecting the complex ways history is taught and remembered globally.

What Battle Am I?

1. This battle took place from August 23, 1942, to February 2, 1943, and was one of the deadliest engagements of World War II. It was marked by brutal urban warfare and a devastating winter. The Soviet Union emerged victorious, marking a significant turning point on the Eastern Front.

   a) Battle of Kursk
   b) Battle of Stalingrad
   c) Battle of Moscow

2. Fought between June 4 and June 7, 1942, this naval battle was a decisive victory for the United States against Japan. It is often considered the turning point of the war in the Pacific, where American forces destroyed four Japanese aircraft carriers.

   a) Battle of Midway
   b) Battle of Guadalcanal
   c) Battle of Coral Sea

3. Taking place from December 16, 1944, to January 25, 1945, this was the last major German offensive campaign on the Western Front. The surprise attack aimed to split the Allied forces and capture the vital Belgian port of Antwerp.

   a) Battle of the Bulge
   b) Battle of Normandy
   c) Battle of the Ardennes

4. This battle occurred between October 23 and November 11, 1942, in North Africa. The Allied victory here marked the beginning of the end for the Axis powers in Africa, leading to the retreat of the Afrika Korps.

   a) Battle of Tobruk
   b) Battle of El Alamein
   c) Battle of Gazala

5. From September 17, 1944, to September 25, 1944, Allied forces launched this ambitious operation to capture key bridges in the Netherlands. Despite initial successes, the operation ultimately failed to secure a crossing over the Rhine.

   a) Operation Market Garden
   b) Operation Overlord
   c) Operation Torch

6. This battle, fought from July 17 to August 2, 1943, was the largest tank battle in history. The Soviet Union defeated the German forces, halting their advance into Soviet territory and shifting the momentum on the Eastern Front.

   a) Battle of Leningrad
   b) Battle of Kursk
   c) Battle of Smolensk

7. Taking place from June 6, 1944, to August 1944, this battle marked the beginning of the Allied invasion of Western Europe. It started with a massive amphibious assault on the beaches of Normandy, France.

   a) Battle of Dunkirk
   b) Battle of the Bulge
   c) Battle of Normandy

8. Fought from October 2, 1941, to January 7, 1942, this was the first major defeat of Nazi Germany during World War II. The harsh winter and fierce Soviet resistance led to the failure of Germany's advance on the Soviet capital.

- a) Battle of Stalingrad
- b) Battle of Moscow
- c) Battle of Kursk

9. This battle occurred from February 19 to March 26, 1945, involving fierce fighting between American forces and the Japanese army on a small volcanic island. The iconic photograph of the flag raising on Mount Suribachi was taken during this battle.

- a) Battle of Okinawa
- b) Battle of Iwo Jima
- c) Battle of Guadalcanal

10. Fought between April 16 and May 2, 1945, this was one of the final major offensives of World War II in Europe. Soviet forces launched a massive assault on the German capital, leading to the eventual fall of Berlin and the end of the war in Europe.

- a) Battle of Berlin
- b) Battle of Vienna
- c) Battle of Prague

Answers

1. b) Battle of Stalingrad

- The Battle of Stalingrad was one of the deadliest battles in history, characterized by brutal urban warfare and extreme winter conditions. The Soviet victory marked a significant turning point on the Eastern Front

2. a) Battle of Midway

- The Battle of Midway was a decisive naval battle that shifted the balance of power in the Pacific in favor of the Allies. The U.S. Navy's destruction of four Japanese aircraft carriers was a critical blow to Japan's naval capabilities.

3. a) Battle of the Bulge

- The Battle of the Bulge was the last major German offensive on the Western Front. The surprise attack through the Ardennes forest aimed to split the Allied forces and capture Antwerp but ultimately failed.

4. b) Battle of El Alamein

- The Battle of El Alamein was a crucial victory for the Allies in North Africa. It marked the beginning of the end for the Axis powers in the region and led to the retreat of the Afrika Korps.

5. a) Operation Market Garden

- Operation Market Garden was an ambitious Allied operation to capture key bridges in the Netherlands. Despite initial successes, the failure to secure a bridge over the Rhine resulted in the operation's overall failure.

6. b) Battle of Kursk

- The Battle of Kursk was the largest tank battle in history. The Soviet victory halted the German advance and shifted the momentum on the Eastern Front in favor of the Allies.

7. c) Battle of Normandy

- The Battle of Normandy, starting with the D-Day landings, was the beginning of the Allied invasion of Western Europe. The successful beach landings and subsequent battles led to the liberation of France.

8. b) Battle of Moscow

- The Battle of Moscow was a significant defeat for Nazi Germany. The harsh winter and determined Soviet defense halted the German advance on the Soviet capital.

9. b) Battle of Iwo Jima

- The Battle of Iwo Jima involved fierce fighting on a small volcanic island. The iconic flag-raising photograph symbolized American bravery and the strategic importance of the island in the Pacific campaign.

10. a) Battle of Berlin

- The Battle of Berlin was the final major offensive in Europe. Soviet forces captured the German capital, leading to the surrender of Nazi Germany and the end of World War II in Europe.

Gandhi's Message of Peace to Hitler

During World War II, Mahatma Gandhi, the iconic leader of the Indian independence movement, extended his philosophy of non-violence and peace beyond his struggle against British colonial rule. Known globally for his commitment to pacifism, Gandhi made a surprising and bold attempt to communicate with Adolf Hitler, one of history's most notorious dictators. In this effort, Gandhi wrote letters to Hitler, addressing him as a 'dear friend' and urging him to cease his aggressive actions and bring an end to the devastating war.

At the time, India was under British rule, and the Indian National Congress, led by Gandhi, was intensifying its efforts to gain independence. The outbreak of World War II added a complex layer to India's political landscape. While the British Indian Army was heavily involved in the war, Gandhi and other Indian leaders were focused on securing India's freedom. The war further fueled the Indian demand for self-governance, as many Indians questioned why they should fight for British interests when their own country was still under colonial subjugation.

Gandhi's first letter to Hitler, dated July 23, 1939, was a plea for peace just before the war began. In this letter, Gandhi implored Hitler to avoid war, suggesting that it would only lead to unnecessary suffering. Gandhi's approach was unique; he addressed Hitler respectfully, in line with his belief in treating everyone, even adversaries, with dignity and respect. He signed the letter as "your sincere friend," reflecting his hope that even the most hardened individuals could be influenced by appeals to their better nature.

In a second letter dated December 24, 1940, Gandhi renewed his appeal after the war had begun. This time, his message was even more urgent, as Europe was already embroiled in conflict. Gandhi's tone was one of desperation and compassion, emphasizing the futility of war and the immense suffering it caused. However, due to the British authorities' censorship, it is unclear if these letters ever reached Hitler.

Though it is doubtful that Hitler ever read Gandhi's letters, the attempts themselves are significant. They underscore Gandhi's unwavering commitment to non-violence and his belief in the power of dialogue and moral persuasion. Even in the face of immense evil, Gandhi maintained his principles, showcasing his extraordinary courage and consistency. These letters are a testament to Gandhi's philosophy that peace and love could triumph over hatred and violence.

India's participation in World War II had a profound impact on its independence movement. The Quit India Movement, launched by Gandhi in 1942, was a direct response to India being dragged into the war without its leaders' consent. The war exacerbated economic difficulties in India, leading to widespread discontent. Gandhi's efforts, both in the struggle for independence and his messages of peace, continued to inspire millions around the world, cementing his legacy as a symbol of non-violent resistance.

- **Albert Einstein to President Franklin D. Roosevelt:** Though not directly to Hitler, Einstein's letter to Roosevelt warned of Nazi Germany's potential to develop atomic weapons, urging the United States to accelerate its own research, leading to the Manhattan Project.
- **King George VI to Adolf Hitler:** Before the war, King George VI attempted to maintain peace by engaging diplomatically with Hitler, sending messages urging for peaceful resolutions.
- **Pope Pius XII to Adolf Hitler:** The Pope tried to use his influence to appeal to Hitler for peace and the humane treatment of prisoners and civilians during the war, emphasizing Christian morals and ethics.

A Commander's Collapse: Himmler's Retreat to a Spa

World War II was not only a time of intense physical battles but also of immense psychological pressure on those in leadership roles. One of the most startling examples of this pressure is the story of Heinrich Himmler, a high-ranking Nazi official who, overwhelmed by his responsibilities, abandoned his post and sought solace at a spa.

Heinrich Himmler was one of Adolf Hitler's earliest supporters and a key architect of the Nazi regime's most heinous policies. As the head of the Schutzstaffel (SS), Himmler was responsible for overseeing the concentration camps and implementing the Final Solution. His rise to power was marked by his ruthless efficiency and unwavering loyalty to Hitler, which eventually led to his appointment as the commander of Army Group Vistula.

By early 1945, Germany was facing inevitable defeat. Army Group Vistula, a force of approximately 500,000 soldiers, was tasked with defending Berlin from the advancing Soviet forces. This was an enormous responsibility, and the pressure to succeed was immense. However, Himmler was ill-suited for the rigors of frontline command. Known for his bureaucratic style and lack of military experience, he struggled under the weight of his new role.

Himmler's inability to cope with the demands of his position became apparent quickly. He required daily naps and massages to manage his stress and only worked a few hours each day. This lack of effective leadership contributed to the deteriorating situation on the Eastern Front. As the Soviet forces advanced,

Army Group Vistula was overwhelmed, and the defense of Berlin became increasingly untenable.

Faced with the collapse of his command, Himmler made a drastic and controversial decision. He abandoned his post and fled to the Hohenlychen Sanatorium, a spa known for its relaxing treatments. This act of desertion was a clear indication of his inability to handle the pressure. At the sanatorium, Himmler attempted to recover from his stress and sought a respite from the war's harsh realities.

While at the spa, Himmler made a surprising move. He tried to negotiate a peace treaty with the advancing Allied forces, hoping to secure a favorable outcome for himself and perhaps for Germany. This effort was not only unsuccessful but also highlighted the desperate and erratic state of Nazi leadership in the war's final days. Himmler's actions were seen as a betrayal by Hitler, leading to his eventual arrest by his own SS troops.

Himmler's retreat to the spa and his failed attempt at peace negotiations did nothing to alter the course of the war. Berlin fell to the Soviets, and the Nazi regime crumbled. Himmler was captured by Allied forces shortly after Germany's surrender and committed suicide while in British custody to avoid standing trial for his war crimes.

Adolf Hitler's Life Through His Quotes

"The victor will never be asked if he told the truth."

This quote reflects Hitler's belief in the primacy of power and victory over morality and truth. Born on April 20, 1889, in Braunau am Inn, Austria, Hitler's early life was marked by a series of personal failures and a deepening resentment towards society. His time in Vienna, where he struggled as an artist and lived in poverty, profoundly shaped his anti-Semitic and nationalist ideologies. These beliefs would later form the foundation of his political ambitions and his rise to power.

"He alone, who owns the youth, gains the future."

Hitler's emphasis on indoctrinating the young is encapsulated in this quote. After serving in World War I and experiencing the harsh conditions of the trenches, Hitler joined the German Workers' Party, which later became the Nazi Party. He focused on creating a youth movement that would secure the future of his ideology. The Hitler Youth became a crucial part of Nazi Germany, training young people in Nazi principles and preparing them for future roles in the regime.

"The great masses of the people will more easily fall victims to a big lie than to a small one."

This quote exemplifies Hitler's understanding of propaganda and mass psychology. As he rose to power, Hitler and his propaganda minister, Joseph Goebbels, employed mass rallies, films, and posters to manipulate public opinion. The Nazi regime's ability to disseminate the "big lie" – an audacious falsehood repeated often enough that it becomes accepted as truth – was key to its control over German society and the perpetuation of its genocidal policies.

"Strength lies not in defense but in attack."

Hitler's aggressive expansionist policy is reflected in this quote. Once in power, Hitler violated the Treaty of Versailles by rebuilding Germany's military and pursuing territorial expansion. His invasions of Poland, France, and the Soviet Union were driven by his belief in Lebensraum, or "living space," for the Aryan race. This strategy of relentless offense led to the widespread devastation of World War II and the initial successes of the Blitzkrieg tactics.

"Anyone can deal with victory. Only the mighty can bear defeat."

This quote ironically underscores Hitler's inability to handle the eventual downfall of the Third Reich. Despite early victories, the tide of the war turned against Nazi Germany with significant defeats like the Battle of Stalingrad and the Allied invasion of Normandy. Hitler's refusal to retreat or acknowledge strategic errors led to catastrophic losses for Germany and hastened the collapse of his regime.

"Make the lie big, make it simple, keep saying it, and eventually they will believe it."

Hitler's propaganda strategy, rooted in this quote, was essential to maintaining his power. The regime's propaganda machine continuously spread falsehoods about the Jews, communists, and other enemies of the state, inciting hatred and justifying the Holocaust. The systematic dissemination of lies ensured public compliance and masked the atrocities committed by the Nazis.

> **"Humanitarianism is the expression of stupidity and cowardice."**

This quote reflects Hitler's disdain for compassion and his justification for the brutal policies of the Nazi regime. His worldview was based on a ruthless application of Social Darwinism, where only the "strongest" deserved to survive and thrive. This philosophy underpinned the horrific acts of genocide, war crimes, and the oppression of countless people deemed inferior by the Nazi ideology.

> **"The art of leadership... consists in consolidating the attention of the people against a single adversary and taking care that nothing will split up that attention."**

Hitler's ability to unite Germany against perceived enemies was a cornerstone of his rule. By blaming Jews, communists, and other minorities for Germany's problems, he created a unified nationalistic fervor. This scapegoating was instrumental in justifying the regime's repressive measures and consolidating Hitler's control over the German population.

> **"Those who want to live, let them fight; and those who do not want to fight in this world of eternal struggle do not deserve to live."**

Hitler's glorification of struggle and conflict is evident in this quote. His worldview was one of perpetual war, where survival depended on one's ability to dominate others. This philosophy justified not only his external wars of conquest but also the internal purges and brutal policies that targeted any opposition within Germany.

> *"It is not truth that matters, but victory."*

This quote encapsulates Hitler's cynical approach to politics and war. His disregard for truth and morality in favor of achieving his goals led to some of the darkest chapters in human history. Hitler's focus on victory at all costs resulted in immense suffering, destruction, and the loss of millions of lives during the Holocaust and World War II.

Did you know?

Before becoming the Führer, Adolf Hitler served as a soldier in World War I, where he was awarded the Iron Cross for bravery. His experiences in the trenches deeply influenced his extreme nationalist and militaristic views, shaping his future policies and ambitions for Germany.

D-Day (Normandy Invasion) Fact File

Date of Invasion: D-Day occurred on June 6, 1944, marking the beginning of Operation Overlord, the Allied invasion of Nazi-occupied Western Europe during World War II.

Largest Amphibious Assault: D-Day remains the largest amphibious military assault in history, involving over 156,000 Allied troops from the United States, United Kingdom, Canada, and other nations.

Beaches Code Names: The five landing beaches were code-named Utah, Omaha, Gold, Juno, and Sword. Each beach was assigned to different Allied forces.

Paratrooper Operations: In addition to the beach landings, approximately 24,000 Allied airborne troops were dropped behind enemy lines to secure key positions and disrupt German defenses.

Deception Plan: The Allies executed a massive deception plan, Operation Fortitude, to mislead the Germans into believing the invasion would occur at Pas de Calais, the narrowest point between Britain and France.

High Casualties: The Allies faced heavy resistance, especially at Omaha Beach, resulting in significant casualties, with estimates of around 4,000-9,000 Allied troops killed, wounded, or missing by the end of the day.

Mulberry Harbors: The Allies constructed two artificial harbors, known as Mulberry Harbors, to facilitate the rapid offloading of cargo onto the beaches, crucial for maintaining the momentum of the invasion.

Allied Air Superiority: The Allies achieved air superiority before the invasion, conducting extensive bombing campaigns to destroy German defenses and infrastructure, aiding the success of the landings.

French Resistance Role: The French Resistance played a crucial role by sabotaging German railways, communication lines, and transport networks, hindering the German ability to reinforce their coastal defenses.

Turning Point: D-Day was a pivotal moment in World War II, leading to the liberation of Western Europe from Nazi control and contributing significantly to the eventual defeat of Germany in May 1945.

Italian Fascism and Italy during WW2 Quiz

1. Which event in 1922 marked the rise of Mussolini to power in Italy?

    a) March on Rome
    b) Battle of Caporetto
    c) Treaty of Versailles

2. What was the name of the paramilitary wing of the Fascist Party in Italy, known for its black uniforms?

    a) Blackshirts
    b) Redshirts
    c) Green Berets

3. Who was the King of Italy who appointed Mussolini as Prime Minister?

    a) Victor Emmanuel II
    b) Victor Emmanuel III
    c) Umberto I

4. Which African country did Italy invade in 1935, leading to international condemnation?

    a) Libya
    b) Ethiopia
    c) Egypt

5. What was the primary reason for Italy's initial military failures during World War II?

    a) Superior enemy technology
    b) Lack of preparation and poor leadership
    c) Unfavorable weather conditions

6. Which significant 1943 event led to the downfall of Mussolini's regime?

- a) Invasion of Sicily
- b) Battle of El Alamein
- c) Bombing of Rome

7. After Mussolini was deposed in 1943, what was the name of the puppet state he led in Northern Italy under German control?

- a) Republic of Italy
- b) Italian Social Republic
- c) Kingdom of Italy

8. What was the role of the Partisans in Italy during World War II?

- a) They supported Mussolini's regime
- b) They were German allies
- c) They resisted Nazi and Fascist forces

9. Which 1944 battle marked the Allied liberation of Rome?

- a) Battle of Monte Cassino
- b) Battle of Anzio
- c) Battle of Salerno

10. How did Mussolini meet his end in April 1945?

- a) He was captured and executed by Italian partisans
- b) He fled to Switzerland and died in exile
- c) He was killed in an air raid

Answers

1. a) March on Rome

- The March on Rome took place in October 1922 and marked the rise of Mussolini to power. Fascist Blackshirts marched to Rome, demanding that King Victor Emmanuel III appoint Mussolini as Prime Minister. The King acquiesced, and Mussolini was able to establish his dictatorship.

2. a) Blackshirts

- The Blackshirts, or "Squadristi," were the paramilitary wing of the Fascist Party in Italy. Known for their black uniforms, they were used to intimidate and violently suppress Mussolini's political opponents, playing a key role in his consolidation of power.

3. b) Victor Emmanuel III

- King Victor Emmanuel III was the monarch who appointed Mussolini as Prime Minister in 1922. His decision was influenced by the fear of civil unrest and the desire to stabilize Italy through Mussolini's strong leadership.

4. b) Ethiopia

- Italy invaded Ethiopia in 1935, an act of aggression that led to international condemnation and strained relations with other nations. The invasion was part of Mussolini's expansionist ambitions to create a new Roman Empire.

5. b) Lack of preparation and poor leadership

- Italy's initial military failures during World War II were primarily due to a lack of preparation and poor leadership. Mussolini's regime overestimated its military capabilities, leading to significant defeats in North Africa, Greece, and other fronts.

6. a) Invasion of Sicily

- The Allied invasion of Sicily in July 1943 was a turning point that led to the downfall of Mussolini's regime. The invasion weakened Mussolini's position, leading to his arrest and the collapse of his government shortly thereafter.

7. b) Italian Social Republic

- After being deposed in 1943, Mussolini was rescued by German forces and installed as the head of the Italian Social Republic, a puppet state in Northern Italy. This regime existed under German control until the end of the war.

8. c) They resisted Nazi and Fascist forces

- The Partisans in Italy were resistance fighters who opposed Nazi and Fascist forces. They played a crucial role in guerrilla warfare and sabotage operations, contributing to the eventual liberation of Italy.

9. b) Battle of Anzio

- The Battle of Anzio was a significant campaign that led to the Allied liberation of Rome in June 1944. The successful landing and subsequent battles allowed the Allies to advance and free the Italian capital from Axis control.

10. a) He was captured and executed by Italian partisans

- Mussolini was captured by Italian partisans on April 27, 1945, as he attempted to flee to Switzerland. He was executed the next day, and his body was displayed publicly in Milan, marking the definitive end of his regime.

Ion Antonescu: The Tyrant of Romania

Ion Victor Antonescu was born on June 15, 1882, in Pitești, Romania. From a young age, Antonescu showed a strong interest in the military, which led him to attend the prestigious Military School in Craiova and later the Higher War School in Bucharest. His early military career was marked by rapid promotions and a reputation for being a disciplined and determined officer. He quickly rose through the ranks, earning respect and recognition within the Romanian army.

By the time World War II began, Antonescu had become a key figure in Romanian military and political circles. In 1940, he seized power by forcing King Carol II into exile, taking advantage of the chaotic political situation and the widespread dissatisfaction with the king's rule. With the king gone, Antonescu appointed himself Conducător (Leader) of Romania, positioning himself as the nation's dictator.

Antonescu was a staunch anti-communist and sympathized with the Nazi ideology, particularly their mission to "purge" the world of Jews and other "undesirable" groups. He saw an alliance with Nazi Germany as an opportunity to strengthen Romania and reclaim territories lost to neighboring countries. In November 1940, he officially allied Romania with the Axis powers, securing military and economic support from Hitler.

Brutal Policies and Massacres

Under Ion Antonescu's rule, Romania became a critical ally of Nazi Germany and a major contributor to the Holocaust. Antonescu's regime was characterized by extreme brutality, particularly towards Jews, Roma, and other minority groups. His collaboration with the Nazis was driven by a blend of ideological alignment and a strategic desire to secure Romania's position within the Axis powers.

Antonescu's anti-Semitic policies were implemented swiftly and ruthlessly. One of his first actions was to enact laws that stripped Jews of their civil rights, expropriated their property, and restricted their access to education and employment. Jewish businesses were confiscated, and Jews were banned from practicing certain professions. These laws aimed to marginalize the Jewish population economically and socially, setting the stage for further persecution.

The regime's brutality escalated with the establishment of ghettos and concentration camps. Jews were rounded up and forced into overcrowded, unsanitary ghettos where disease and starvation were rampant. In regions such as Bessarabia and Bukovina, which were under Romanian control, mass deportations and executions became commonplace. The infamous Iași pogrom in June 1941 saw the massacre of at least 13,000 Jews by Romanian soldiers and police.

Antonescu also targeted the Roma population, subjecting them to similar atrocities. Thousands of Roma were deported to the Transnistria region, a territory occupied by Romania in present-day Ukraine. There, they faced brutal conditions, including forced labor, inadequate shelter, and scarce food supplies. Many perished from starvation, disease, or outright execution.

The scale of the massacres orchestrated by Antonescu's regime was staggering. During his rule, approximately 300,000 Jews and up to 100,000 members of other ethnicities, including Roma and ethnic Ukrainians, were murdered in Romania and the territories it controlled. These acts of genocide were carried out with chilling efficiency, often with the direct involvement of Romanian military and police forces.

Despite his ruthless policies, Antonescu displayed a contradictory pragmatism regarding the Jewish population within "Old Romania"—the core Romanian territories excluding the occupied regions. Recognizing their economic value, he allowed many Jews in these areas to live and continue working, resisting Hitler's demands to deport them to Nazi death camps. This decision, driven by economic considerations rather than humanitarian concerns, added a complex layer to his otherwise brutal regime.

Military Campaigns

Romania's military, under Antonescu's command, played a significant role in supporting Nazi Germany's war efforts. Antonescu's strategic alliance with Hitler was motivated by a desire to expand Romania's influence and recover territories lost after World War I. Romanian troops were heavily involved in several key campaigns on the Eastern Front, fighting alongside German forces in some of the war's most brutal battles.

One of the earliest and most significant contributions of Romanian forces was during Operation Barbarossa, the German invasion of the Soviet Union in June 1941. Romanian troops participated in the Siege of Odessa, a critical battle aimed at capturing the strategic port city. The siege lasted from August to October 1941 and was marked by intense urban combat. Romanian forces, alongside German units, faced fierce resistance from Soviet defenders. The capture of Odessa, although eventually successful, came at a high cost, with significant Romanian casualties.

Following the fall of Odessa, Romanian troops were involved in the occupation and administration of the Transnistria region. This occupation saw the continuation of brutal anti-Semitic policies, with mass executions and deportations becoming routine. The region served as a grim laboratory for Antonescu's genocidal ambitions, with concentration camps and ghettos established to systematically exterminate the local Jewish and Roma populations.

Romanian forces also played a pivotal role in the Battle of Stalingrad, one of the most significant and grueling confrontations of World War II. In the fall of 1942, Romanian armies were deployed to the flanks of the German 6th Army, tasked with protecting them from Soviet counterattacks. Despite their determination, the Romanian troops were poorly equipped and ill-prepared for the harsh winter conditions and the relentless Soviet offensives.

The Soviet counteroffensive, Operation Uranus, launched in November 1942, targeted the weaker Romanian forces guarding the flanks. The Romanian lines quickly collapsed under the weight of the assault, leading to the encirclement of the German 6th Army in Stalingrad. The defeat at Stalingrad was catastrophic for both the Germans and their Romanian allies, marking a turning point in the war and signaling the beginning of the Axis powers' decline on the Eastern Front.

Despite the devastating losses, Antonescu remained committed to the Nazi cause. He continued to send Romanian troops and resources to support German operations, driven by a belief that a German victory would secure Romania's territorial ambitions. This unwavering support persisted even as the war turned increasingly against the Axis powers.

Romanian forces were involved in several other key battles, including the offensives in the Caucasus and the defense of the Crimean Peninsula. These campaigns further strained Romania's military capabilities and inflicted heavy casualties on its troops. The relentless fighting, coupled with the harsh conditions and strong Soviet resistance, eroded the morale and effectiveness of Romanian forces.

Decline and Fall

As World War II progressed and the tide turned against the Axis powers, Ion Antonescu's grip on power in Romania became increasingly tenuous. The Soviet Union's relentless advance into Eastern Europe, coupled with significant defeats suffered by Romanian troops on the Eastern Front, severely undermined Antonescu's authority. By 1944, the Red Army was pushing into Romanian territory, signaling an imminent occupation. The disastrous Battle of Stalingrad and subsequent Soviet offensives had decimated Romanian forces, eroding both their fighting capacity and morale. These military setbacks, along with growing domestic discontent, made Antonescu's position precarious.

The situation in Romania grew dire as the Red Army approached. Recognizing the inevitability of Soviet occupation, and the need to align with the winning side, King Michael I, supported by anti-fascist politicians and military leaders, orchestrated a coup on August 23, 1944. The coup was executed with precision: Antonescu was swiftly arrested and his government was overthrown. This sudden change in leadership facilitated Romania's switch of allegiance from the Axis to the Allies, significantly hastening the end of the war in Eastern Europe. Antonescu, once a powerful dictator, found himself a prisoner of the very forces he had sought to suppress.

Following his arrest, Antonescu was handed over to the Soviet authorities and later extradited to Romania. There, he faced a trial for war crimes and crimes against humanity. The Romanian People's Tribunal, established to prosecute those responsible for wartime atrocities, took on his case. Antonescu's trial was a high-profile event, drawing significant attention both domestically and internationally. During the proceedings, he was held accountable for the systematic massacre of Jews, Roma, and other minorities under his regime. Despite his defense, which included claims of mitigating actions such as his refusal to deport Romanian Jews to Nazi death camps, the evidence against him was overwhelming.

The court found Ion Antonescu guilty of orchestrating and implementing policies that led to the deaths of hundreds of thousands of people. His brutal reign, marked by genocide and collaboration with Nazi Germany, left a deep scar on Romania's history. In 1946, the tribunal sentenced Antonescu to death. The verdict was a reflection of the immense suffering inflicted upon the Romanian people and the broader atrocities of the Holocaust. Antonescu's sentence underscored the need for justice and the reckoning with the horrific consequences of his regime.

On June 1, 1946, Ion Antonescu was executed by firing squad at Jilava Prison near Bucharest. His execution marked the symbolic end of a dark and brutal chapter in Romanian history. However, the legacy of his regime's atrocities continued to haunt the nation. The systematic extermination of Jews, Roma, and other minorities under his rule remains one of the most harrowing episodes of the Holocaust. Antonescu's fall from power and subsequent execution served as a stark reminder of the destructive impact of totalitarianism and the importance of accountability for crimes against humanity.

P.S. I must confess, (sorry Romanian readers), I didn't know too much about Romania's modern history. Anyway, here are some crazy facts I found along my research of Ion Antonescu:

- **The Iron Guard**: A fascist, far-right organization in Romania that initially allied with Antonescu but was later suppressed by him. Their extreme violence and radical nationalism left a lasting impact on the country's political landscape.
- **Operation Tidal Wave**: A massive bombing campaign by the Allies targeting Romanian oil refineries in Ploiești in 1943. The operation was one of the most daring and costly air raids of the war, aiming to cripple the Axis oil supply.
- **Transnistria Governorate**: An area in present-day Ukraine that was occupied and administered by Romania during WWII. It became a site of horrific massacres and deportations, with ghettos and concentration camps established under Antonescu's orders.
- **Romanian Royal Coup**: The 1944 coup that deposed Antonescu was led by King Michael I, who later received international recognition for his role in switching Romania's allegiance to the Allies, significantly impacting the war's Eastern Front.
- **Prisoners of War**: After WWII, many Romanian soldiers who fought alongside the Nazis were captured by the Soviets and sent to labor camps. The return of these soldiers years later contributed to the complex post-war rehabilitation of Romania.

- **Communist Takeover**: Following WWII and the deposition of Antonescu, Romania fell under Soviet influence and eventually became a communist state in 1947, drastically changing the nation's political and social landscape for decades.
- **Decree 770**: Enacted by the communist regime in 1966, this decree aimed to increase the birthrate by banning abortion and contraception. It had profound and often tragic consequences for Romanian society.
- **Ceaușescu's Cult of Personality**: Nicolae Ceaușescu, the communist leader who ruled Romania from 1965 to 1989, developed an extensive cult of personality, leading to severe economic mismanagement and widespread human rights abuses.
- **1989 Revolution**: The anti-communist revolution in December 1989 led to the overthrow and execution of Nicolae Ceaușescu, ending decades of repressive communist rule and paving the way for Romania's transition to democracy.
- **Modern NATO Membership**: Romania joined NATO in 2004, marking a significant shift in its international alliances and signaling its integration into the Western military and political sphere.
- **EU Membership**: Romania became a member of the European Union in 2007, which has led to significant economic growth, increased foreign investment, and improved infrastructure across the country.
- **Bucharest's Tech Boom**: The capital city, Bucharest, has become a burgeoning tech hub in Eastern Europe, attracting numerous international tech companies and fostering a vibrant start-up culture.

Charles de Gaulle's Life Through His Quotes

> *"France has lost a battle. But France has not lost the war."*

This quote encapsulates Charles de Gaulle's unwavering spirit and determination during World War II. Born on November 22, 1890, in Lille, France, de Gaulle's early life was marked by a strong sense of patriotism and duty. He pursued a military career, serving with distinction during World War I. His boldness and vision for France's future set the stage for his later roles as a leader of the Free French Forces and the architect of modern France.

> *"I have come to the conclusion that politics is too serious a matter to be left to the politicians."*

De Gaulle's belief in active and principled leadership is reflected in this quote. After the fall of France in 1940, he fled to Britain and famously rallied the French people through his broadcasts from London. He established the Free French Forces, refusing to accept the Vichy government's collaboration with Nazi Germany. De Gaulle's commitment to France's sovereignty and his vision for a free and democratic France inspired many to resist and fight for liberation.

> *"Greatness is a road leading towards the unknown."*

This quote epitomizes de Gaulle's forward-thinking and resilient nature. Throughout his career, he faced numerous setbacks, including political exile and opposition. Despite these challenges, his resilience remained unwavering, particularly during the "wilderness years" when he was out of favor politically. His steadfastness in the face of adversity became a defining trait of his leadership, especially during the turbulent times following World War II.

"Deliberation is the work of many men. Action, of one alone."

De Gaulle's pragmatic view of leadership is highlighted in this quote. His leadership during the liberation of France exemplified this philosophy. After Paris was liberated in 1944, de Gaulle led the Provisional Government, focusing on restoring order and rebuilding the nation. Despite the complexities of post-war politics, de Gaulle's decisive actions were crucial in stabilizing France and setting the groundwork for its recovery.

"No nation has friends, only interests."

This quote from de Gaulle reflects his realistic approach to international relations and his focus on France's national interests. His ability to communicate the importance of French sovereignty and independence was a key aspect of his leadership. De Gaulle's policies often emphasized France's distinct path in the global arena, balancing relations with both the United States and the Soviet Union during the Cold War.

"Patriotism is when love of your own people comes first; nationalism, when hate for people other than your own comes first."

De Gaulle believed in a strong, united France that respected and cooperated with other nations. His leadership in founding the Fifth

Republic in 1958 and his role as its first President were pivotal moments where his vision for a stable, democratic France was realized. His strategic foresight and dedication to his principles were instrumental in shaping modern France's political landscape.

"Politics is a fierce and violent sport."

De Gaulle's willingness to confront difficult issues and stand up for his beliefs often made him a polarizing figure. His strong opposition to colonialism and his decisions to grant independence to former colonies were initially unpopular but proved prescient. De Gaulle's ability to stand firm in his convictions, despite criticism and opposition, underscored his leadership style and his commitment to his principles.

"You have to be fast on your feet and adaptive or else a strategy is useless."

This quote reflects de Gaulle's philosophy of perseverance and adaptability during challenging times. His leadership during the crises of May 1968, when France faced widespread student and worker protests, exemplified this tenacity. De Gaulle's resolve and his ability to navigate through political turmoil were crucial in maintaining national stability and order.

"In politics it is necessary either to betray one's country or the electorate. I prefer to betray the electorate."

De Gaulle's foresight and vision for the future are encapsulated in this quote. After World War II, he recognized the need for a strong executive branch to guide France through the complexities of the Cold War and the process of decolonization. His advocacy for constitutional reform and his vision for a united Europe highlighted his understanding of the emerging global dynamics and the need for strategic alliances and cooperation.

"History does not teach fatalism. There are moments when the will of a handful of free men breaks through determinism and opens up new roads."

De Gaulle's awareness of his historical legacy is evident in this quote. An accomplished writer and historian, he authored several works, including his memoirs, which documented his experiences and perspectives. His writings not only chronicled his life but also shaped the narrative of 20th-century French history, ensuring his enduring influence and legacy.

Did you know?

Before his prominent role in World War II, Charles de Gaulle gained fame for his military writings and theories on armored warfare, which were ahead of their time. His early advocacy for mobile armored divisions and mechanized warfare significantly influenced French military doctrine, although his ideas were initially met with resistance. His early career and writings set the stage for his later leadership and strategic acumen.

The Nazi Party Quiz

The Nazi Party, officially known as the National Socialist German Workers' Party, was one of the most destructive and infamous political movements in history. Under the leadership of Adolf Hitler, the Nazis perpetrated unimaginable atrocities, including the genocide of six million Jews during the Holocaust and the instigation of World War II, which resulted in the deaths of tens of millions. But do you know the key aspects that defined this malevolent regime? Test your knowledge with our quiz on the Nazi Party, and delve into the events, figures, and policies that shaped its rise and fall.

Questions

1. Which event in 1933 marked the consolidation of Hitler's power, allowing him to rule by decree?

- a) Reichstag Fire
- b) Night of the Long Knives
- c) Beer Hall Putsch

2. What was the name of the paramilitary wing of the Nazi Party, often involved in violent street clashes?

- a) SS (Schutzstaffel)
- b) SA (Sturmabteilung)
- c) Gestapo

3. Who was the head of the Nazi propaganda machine, responsible for spreading Nazi ideology?

- a) Heinrich Himmler
- b) Joseph Goebbels
- c) Hermann Göring

4. Which symbol became the emblem of the Nazi Party?

   a) Iron Cross
   b) Swastika
   c) Eagle of the Third Reich

5. What was the name of the Nazi policy aimed at unifying all German-speaking people?

   a) Lebensraum
   b) Anschluss
   c) Gleichschaltung

6. Which 1935 laws institutionalized racial discrimination against Jews in Nazi Germany?

   a) Enabling Acts
   b) Nuremberg Laws
   c) Final Solution

7. Who was the commander of the Luftwaffe, the German air force under the Nazi regime?

   a) Erwin Rommel
   b) Heinrich Himmler
   c) Hermann Göring

8. What was the purpose of the Hitler Youth (Hitlerjugend)?

   a) To prepare boys for military service and instill Nazi ideology
   b) To serve as a paramilitary organization
   c) To act as a secret police force

9. Which book, written by Hitler, outlines the ideological foundation of the Nazi Party?

   a) Mein Kampf
   b) Das Kapital
   c) Der Führer

10. **What was the main goal of the Kristallnacht (Night of Broken Glass) in 1938?**

   a) To celebrate Nazi victories
   b) To instigate a mass attack on Jewish communities and properties
   c) To commemorate the founding of the Nazi Party

Answers

1. a) Reichstag Fire

- The Reichstag Fire occurred on February 27, 1933, and was blamed on a Dutch communist, Marinus van der Lubbe. This event was used by Hitler to justify the Reichstag Fire Decree, which suspended civil liberties and allowed the arrest of political opponents, consolidating his power.

2. b) SA (Sturmabteilung)

- The SA, also known as the Brownshirts, were instrumental in Hitler's rise to power, often engaging in violent clashes with political opponents. They were later purged during the Night of the Long Knives in 1934, reducing their influence in favor of the SS.

3. b) Joseph Goebbels

- Joseph Goebbels was the Minister of Propaganda and was highly effective in using media, including films, radio, and literature, to spread Nazi ideology and maintain control over public opinion.

4. b) Swastika

- The swastika was adopted by the Nazi Party in the 1920s as a symbol of Aryan identity and German nationalist pride. It became one of the most recognized symbols of the Nazi regime.

5. b) Anschluss

- Anschluss refers to the annexation of Austria into Nazi Germany in 1938, a move that was part of Hitler's goal to unite all German-speaking peoples under one nation. It was accomplished without military conflict, largely through political pressure and propaganda.

6. b) Nuremberg Laws

- Enacted in 1935, the Nuremberg Laws included the Reich Citizenship Law and the Law for the Protection of German Blood and German Honor, which severely restricted the rights of Jews and laid the groundwork for their systematic persecution.

7. c) Hermann Göring

- Hermann Göring was a leading member of the Nazi Party and a close ally of Hitler. As commander of the Luftwaffe, he played a crucial role in the early successes of the German military, though his leadership later faced criticism due to the Luftwaffe's failures.

8. a) To prepare boys for military service and instill Nazi ideology

- The Hitler Youth was established to indoctrinate young Germans with Nazi beliefs and prepare them for future roles in the military and society. By 1939, membership was compulsory for all eligible youths.

9. a) Mein Kampf

- "Mein Kampf," meaning "My Struggle," was written by Hitler during his imprisonment following the failed Beer Hall Putsch. It outlines his political ideology and plans for Germany's future, including his views on race and expansionism.

10. b) To instigate a mass attack on Jewish communities and properties

- Kristallnacht, or the Night of Broken Glass, took place on November 9-10, 1938. It involved the widespread destruction of Jewish businesses, synagogues, and homes, and marked a significant escalation in the Nazi campaign against Jews, leading to increased persecution and deportations.

Kristallnacht, resulted in the destruction of over 7,000 Jewish businesses, the burning of more than 1,400 synagogues, and the death of approximately 91 Jews. The name "Kristallnacht" comes from the shards of broken glass that littered the streets following the vandalism and destruction. This pogrom marked a significant escalation in the Nazi regime's anti-Semitic policies, leading to the arrest of about 30,000 Jewish men who were sent to concentration camps. The international response to Kristallnacht was one of widespread condemnation, but it also highlighted the world's limited action against the growing threat of Nazi aggression. The event is often seen as a prelude to the Holocaust, illustrating the regime's increasing willingness to use violence against Jews.

Did You Know?

In present-day Germany, the public display of the swastika and other Nazi symbols is strictly prohibited by law. This ban, established to prevent the resurgence of neo-Nazi ideologies and to honor the victims of the Holocaust, is enforced under the German Criminal Code. Exceptions to this rule are made only for educational purposes, such as in historical documentaries, books, or museums that aim to provide context about World War II and the atrocities committed by the Nazi regime. Violating this law can lead to severe penalties, including fines and imprisonment, reflecting Germany's commitment to confronting its past and promoting a society free from hate and intolerance.

In addition to the swastika, Germany also bans a variety of other symbols and practices associated with the Nazi era. These include the

SS runes, the Nazi salute, and any gestures or phrases that promote the ideology of National Socialism. The production, distribution, or public wearing of Nazi uniforms and paraphernalia is also illegal. The laws extend to digital spaces, prohibiting the dissemination of Nazi propaganda and hate speech online. Germany's approach is part of a broader effort to combat right-wing extremism, which also includes educational programs, memorials, and strict enforcement of hate crime laws. This comprehensive framework aims to ensure that the horrors of the past are not forgotten and that such ideologies do not take root again.

Battle of Stalingrad

The Battle of Stalingrad, fought between August 23, 1942, and February 2, 1943, is widely regarded as one of the most brutal and pivotal battles of World War II. It marked a significant turning point in the conflict, halting the German advance into the Soviet Union and beginning the pushback that would eventually lead to the fall of Nazi Germany.

Stalingrad, now known as Volgograd, was a key industrial city on the Volga River, crucial for both its strategic location and its symbolic value, as it bore the name of Soviet leader Joseph Stalin. The battle began with a massive German offensive led by General Friedrich Paulus's 6th Army and elements of the 4th Panzer Army. The German strategy, known as Operation Blue, aimed to capture the oil-rich Caucasus region and cut off Soviet transport along the Volga.

The initial German assault involved intense aerial bombardments that reduced much of the city to rubble. However, this destruction created a chaotic urban battlefield where the Germans' superior mobility and tank tactics were less effective. The Soviet defense, under the command of General Vasily Chuikov, employed a strategy of attrition and close-quarters combat, famously known as "hugging the enemy," to negate the German advantage in air power and artillery.

Soviet soldiers defended every street, building, and factory, turning the battle into a grueling fight for every inch of the city.

As the harsh Russian winter set in, the Germans found themselves ill-prepared for the conditions and the tenacity of Soviet resistance. On November 19, 1942, the Soviets launched Operation Uranus, a massive counteroffensive aimed at encircling the German forces. Soviet armies attacked the weaker Romanian and Hungarian units guarding the German flanks, quickly breaking through and encircling the 6th Army in Stalingrad.

Trapped and cut off from supplies, the German forces endured months of relentless Soviet attacks, starvation, and freezing temperatures. Despite Hitler's orders to fight to the last man, Paulus surrendered on February 2, 1943, leading to the capture of approximately 91,000 German troops. The battle resulted in staggering casualties, with estimates of over 2 million dead, wounded, or captured on both sides. The defeat at Stalingrad dealt a severe blow to German morale and military capability, marking the first major defeat of Hitler's forces on the Eastern Front. It significantly weakened the Wehrmacht and shifted the balance of power in favor of the Allies.

The battle is famous for the legendary sniper duel between Soviet sniper Vasily Zaytsev and a supposed German sniper named Major Erwin König. Although the story is popularized in books and films, historical evidence for König's existence is debated. Zaytsev, however, is credited with over 225 confirmed kills during the battle.

Some of the fiercest fighting occurred in the industrial complexes of Stalingrad, such as the Red October factory, the Barrikady Gun Factory, and the Dzerzhinsky Tractor Factory.

The intense urban combat at Stalingrad was referred to by the Germans as "Rattenkrieg" or "Rat War," due to the close-quarters, brutal fighting conditions. Soldiers fought for control of individual rooms, staircases, and even sewer tunnels, turning the city into a maze of deadly engagements.

The success of Operation Uranus, the Soviet counteroffensive, relied heavily on the element of surprise and the weak Axis flanks, manned by Romanian, Hungarian, and Italian troops

In a futile attempt to encourage him to fight on, Hitler promoted Friedrich Paulus to the rank of Field Marshal on January 30, 1943, just days before his surrender. This was symbolic, as no German Field Marshal had ever been captured alive, but Paulus chose to surrender rather than continue a hopeless battle, becoming the first Field Marshal to be taken prisoner.

The Night Witches: Silent Shadows of the Eastern Front

In the dark skies over Nazi-occupied territories, the eerie silence was broken only by the faint rustle of gliding aircraft. German soldiers, straining their ears against the quiet, feared these ghostly intruders—the Soviet Union's 588th Night Bomber Regiment, famously known as the 'Night Witches'. These female pilots struck terror into the hearts of their enemies, performing nocturnal bombing raids with unparalleled courage and stealth.

The 588th Night Bomber Regiment was formed in 1942 as part of the Soviet Union's effort to repel the German invasion. This unique unit was composed entirely of women, a testament to the Soviet commitment to utilizing every resource available, including the often-overlooked potential of female soldiers. The regiment was commanded by Major Marina Raskova, a celebrated aviator known as the "Soviet Amelia Earhart," who played a crucial role in advocating for women's inclusion in combat roles.

The Night Witches flew the Polikarpov Po-2, a biplane originally designed for training and crop-dusting. This seemingly outdated aircraft had the advantage of being exceptionally maneuverable and capable of flying at low altitudes, making it difficult for German radar and fighters to detect. The pilots would fly multiple sorties per night, often as many as eight to ten, carrying bombs that were manually released over enemy targets.

To avoid detection, the women developed a daring tactic: they would cut their engines before reaching their targets, allowing their planes to glide silently through the night. This soundless approach earned them the nickname 'Night Witches' from the Germans, who likened the noise of the wind through the biplanes' wings to the swishing of witches' broomsticks.

Among the many brave pilots was Nadezhda Popova, who flew 852 missions and survived being shot down multiple times. Her story is one of incredible resilience and bravery. On one occasion, after being shot down, she and her navigator managed to evade capture and rejoin their regiment, only to take to the skies again the next night.

The impact of the Night Witches on the war was significant. They were responsible for dropping over 23,000 tons of bombs, disrupting German supply lines and causing considerable chaos and fear among the enemy troops. Their efforts were instrumental in the Soviet war effort, particularly in the battles of the Caucasus and the advance into Eastern Europe.

The legacy of the Night Witches extends beyond their tactical success. They shattered gender stereotypes and proved that women could perform under the most grueling conditions of warfare. Thirty-two Night Witches were awarded the title Hero of the Soviet Union, the nation's highest honor, in recognition of their valor.

- The majority of the Night Witches were young women in their late teens and early twenties. Many of them were barely out of school when they joined the regiment. Despite their youth and limited flying experience, their determination and rigorous training enabled them to become highly effective pilots.
- The Polikarpov Po-2 biplanes used by the Night Witches were incredibly basic, lacking any modern navigation

instruments. The pilots navigated using maps and compasses, often relying on their keen sense of direction and the stars to find their way to and from their targets. This lack of advanced equipment made their missions even more dangerous and required extraordinary skill and bravery.
- Due to the limited payload capacity of their aircraft, the Night Witches employed innovative bombing techniques. They would often carry multiple small bombs and drop them in quick succession to maximize damage and confusion among the enemy. This method, combined with their stealthy approach, made their bombing raids particularly effective in disrupting German operations and causing panic.

Bat Bombs: America's Unconventional Weapon Experiment

In the midst of World War II, the United States military explored a variety of unconventional weapons to gain an edge over their adversaries. Among the most peculiar and ambitious of these experiments was the concept of bat bombs, an idea that sought to turn nature into a devastating weapon against enemy cities. This imaginative project aimed to harness the natural behavior of bats to deliver incendiary devices to Japanese targets, potentially causing widespread destruction.

The idea of bat bombs was conceived by Dr. Lytle S. Adams, a Pennsylvania dentist with a penchant for innovative thinking. Inspired by a trip to Carlsbad Caverns, where he observed millions of bats, Adams envisioned using these nocturnal creatures to deliver incendiary bombs. He proposed the concept to President Franklin D. Roosevelt, who saw potential in the idea and approved further research and development.

The project, officially known as Project X-Ray, involved creating a bomb with over a thousand individual compartments, each housing a hibernating Mexican free-tailed bat. To each bat, a small, timed incendiary device was attached. The plan was to drop these bombs from aircraft over Japanese cities. Upon release, the bats would awaken from hibernation, disperse, and seek out dark, secluded places to roost within the predominantly paper and wood structures of the urban areas.

Initial tests of the bat bombs took place in New Mexico, where a series of controlled releases were conducted to observe the behavior of the bats and the effectiveness of the incendiary devices. The results were mixed; while the bats did indeed roost in buildings, there were several unintended consequences. During one test, some bats escaped prematurely, setting fire to an airbase. Despite these setbacks, the potential of the bat bombs was evident, prompting further refinement and testing.

Several challenges plagued the project, from the difficulty of ensuring the bats remained in hibernation during transport to the complexity of attaching and synchronizing the incendiary devices. Additionally, the unpredictable nature of the bats' flight patterns and roosting behavior made it hard to guarantee that they would target the desired locations. These issues, combined with the rapid advancements in other more conventional weapon technologies, eventually led to the project's decline.

As World War II progressed, the development of the atomic bomb under the Manhattan Project overshadowed other experimental weapon projects, including the bat bombs. By 1944, the bat bomb project was officially abandoned. Although it never saw combat, the project provided valuable insights into unconventional warfare tactics and the potential for biological agents in military applications.

The bat bomb experiment remains one of the most unusual and inventive wartime projects undertaken by the United States. It highlights the lengths to which military planners were willing to go in their quest for new ways to disrupt and defeat the enemy. The story of the bat bombs is a testament to human creativity and the unpredictable nature of innovation during times of conflict.

While the bat bomb project was ultimately deemed impractical, it serves as a fascinating example of unconventional thinking in warfare. It also raises ethical questions about the use of animals in military operations and the unpredictable consequences of such experiments. The legacy of Project X-Ray lives on as a curious footnote in the history of World War II, reminding us of the diverse and often surprising approaches to warfare that have been considered throughout history.

- The British experimented with the idea of building aircraft carriers out of pykrete, a mixture of wood pulp and ice, which was believed to be resistant to conventional bombs and torpedoes. This floating fortress concept was intended to provide a durable and nearly unsinkable platform for aircraft in the North Atlantic.
- Devised by American psychologist B.F. Skinner, this project aimed to use pigeons to guide bombs to their targets. Pigeons were trained to peck at a target image, steering the bomb towards it. Although tests showed promise, the project was eventually shelved in favor of electronic guidance systems.
- The British Special Operations Executive developed a plan to use dead rats filled with explosives. The idea was to place these rats in locations where they would be disposed of in industrial furnaces, causing explosions that could damage machinery or disrupt operations. While the project did not see widespread use, it demonstrated the innovative and sometimes bizarre approaches to sabotage during the war.

Who Am I - Medium

1. I was an American general who played a crucial role in the Pacific Theater during World War II. My famous promise to return to the Philippines became a rallying cry, and I fulfilled this promise, leading Allied forces to liberate the islands.
   Who am I?

   _____

2. I was the British mathematician and logician who played a key role in breaking the German Enigma code. My work at Bletchley Park significantly shortened the war and laid the foundations for modern computer science.
   Who am I?

   _____

3. I was an Italian physicist and Nobel laureate who fled fascist Italy for the United States. My work on neutron moderation was critical to the development of the first nuclear reactor and the atomic bomb.
   Who am I?

   _____

4. I was a Japanese admiral and the mastermind behind the attack on Pearl Harbor. My strategy aimed to cripple the U.S. Pacific Fleet, giving Japan a tactical advantage at the start of the war.
   Who am I?

   _____

5. I was a Chinese military leader and head of the Nationalist Government of China. I led the Chinese resistance against

Japanese invasion during World War II and later became the President of the Republic of China in Taiwan.
Who am I?

Answers

1. **Douglas MacArthur**, born in 1880 in Little Rock, Arkansas, was an American general who played a crucial role in the Pacific Theater during World War II. His famous promise to return to the Philippines became a rallying cry for the Allied forces. MacArthur fulfilled this promise in 1944, leading the liberation of the Philippines from Japanese occupation. His leadership and strategic acumen were instrumental in the Allies' success in the Pacific.

2. **Alan Turing**, born in 1912 in London, England, was a British mathematician and logician who played a key role in breaking the German Enigma code. His work at Bletchley Park, where he developed the Bombe machine to decrypt Enigma-encrypted messages, significantly shortened the war. Turing's contributions laid the foundations for modern computer science and artificial intelligence, and he is celebrated as one of the greatest minds of the 20th century.

3. **Enrico Fermi,** born in 1901 in Rome, Italy, was an Italian physicist and Nobel laureate who fled fascist Italy for the United States. His groundbreaking work on neutron moderation was critical to the development of the first nuclear reactor, known as the Chicago Pile-1, and the atomic bomb as part of the Manhattan Project. Fermi's contributions to nuclear physics and quantum theory have had a lasting impact on science and technology.

4. **Isoroku Yamamoto**, born in 1884 in Nagaoka, Japan, was a Japanese admiral and the mastermind behind the attack on Pearl Harbor. As Commander-in-Chief of the Combined Fleet, Yamamoto aimed to neutralize the U.S. Pacific Fleet, giving Japan a tactical advantage at the start of the war. The surprise attack on December 7, 1941, led to the United States' entry into World War II. Yamamoto's strategic decisions had far-reaching consequences for the Pacific Theater.

5. **Chiang Kai-shek**, born in 1887 in Xikou, China, was a Chinese military leader and head of the Nationalist Government of China. He led the Chinese resistance against the Japanese invasion during World War II and worked closely with Allied powers. After the war, Chiang became the President of the Republic of China in Taiwan, continuing to lead the Nationalist government after the Chinese Civil War. His leadership was pivotal in the fight against Japanese aggression and in shaping modern Taiwan.

Canine Warriors: The Tragic Tale of Soviet Anti-Tank Dogs

In the vast and brutal theaters of World War II, desperation and innovation often intersected in remarkable ways. One of the most poignant and controversial examples of this intersection was the Soviet Union's use of anti-tank dogs. These specially trained dogs were deployed against German tanks and armored vehicles, carrying explosives designed to cripple the enemy's formidable war machines. While the concept showed ingenuity, it also highlighted the tragic costs of warfare.

As the German Wehrmacht advanced into Soviet territory during Operation Barbarossa in 1941, the Red Army faced overwhelming odds. Soviet forces were desperate for effective means to halt the relentless progress of German tanks. Amidst this dire situation, the Soviet military turned to an unconventional solution: training dogs to carry explosives under enemy tanks. The initiative was part of a broader strategy to utilize all available resources to defend the motherland.

The Soviet anti-tank dog program began with rigorous training at specialized schools. Dogs, primarily Alsatians and mixed breeds, were selected for their intelligence and agility. Trainers used a variety of methods to condition the dogs to associate the undersides of tanks with food rewards. Initially, the dogs were equipped with timer-detonated bombs, which allowed them to leave the explosives under the vehicles and run to safety.

In the chaos of battle, these canine warriors were released onto the battlefield with explosive packs strapped to their backs. The dogs were trained to run under the German tanks, where the bombs would then be detached and timed to explode after a short delay. This tactic aimed to damage or destroy the tanks without immediately harming the dogs.

However, as the war progressed and the need for immediate results grew, the Soviets switched to impact-detonated bombs, which would explode upon contact with the tanks, sacrificing the dogs in the process.

The use of anti-tank dogs was fraught with difficulties and ethical concerns. One of the main challenges was that the dogs, often under extreme stress and confusion in battle, sometimes ran back to their handlers or to Soviet tanks, causing unintended casualties. Additionally, the shift to impact-detonated bombs, while operationally more effective, raised significant moral questions about the use of animals in such a lethal and sacrificial manner.

The actual effectiveness of the anti-tank dogs in disabling German tanks remains debated among historians. While there are reports of some successes, the program was not as decisive as the Soviets had hoped. The psychological impact on both Soviet and German troops, however, was notable. The Germans were initially taken aback by this unexpected tactic, which added an element of unpredictability to the battlefield.

The story of the Soviet anti-tank dogs is a somber reminder of the extremes to which nations will go in times of desperate conflict. It reflects the innovative yet often tragic strategies employed during World War II. The legacy of these canine soldiers is remembered with a mixture of admiration for their bravery and sorrow for their fate.

In the annals of World War II history, the use of anti-tank dogs by the Soviet Union stands out as a testament to both the creativity and the tragic desperation of wartime innovation. These canine warriors, trained to face the mechanized monsters of war, symbolize the lengths to which humanity will go in the pursuit of survival and victory. Their story is one of courage, sacrifice, and the complex ethical dilemmas that arise in the heat of battle.

Joseph Stalin's Life Through His Quotes

"A single death is a tragedy; a million deaths is a statistic."

This quote reflects Stalin's stark and often brutal perspective on power and the human cost of his policies. Born on December 18, 1878, in Gori, Georgia, Stalin's early life was marked by hardship and rebellion against the oppressive Russian Empire. Rising through the ranks of the Bolshevik Party, his ruthlessness and political acumen set the stage for his eventual control over the Soviet Union.

"Ideas are more powerful than guns. We would not let our enemies have guns; why should we let them have ideas?"

Stalin's commitment to maintaining absolute control over the Soviet Union is encapsulated in this quote. After Lenin's death in 1924, Stalin systematically eliminated his rivals to consolidate power. His regime was characterized by strict censorship, propaganda, and the suppression of dissent. Stalin believed in the power of ideology to shape society, and he exerted tight control over intellectual and cultural life in the Soviet Union.

> ### *"The people who cast the votes decide nothing. The people who count the votes decide everything."*

This quote epitomizes Stalin's cynical view of democracy and political power. Throughout his rule, Stalin manipulated political processes to maintain his grip on power. He orchestrated purges, show trials, and political repressions to eliminate potential threats and ensure loyalty within the Communist Party. Stalin's totalitarian regime left little room for genuine political opposition or democratic practices.

> ### *"Death solves all problems—no man, no problem."*

Stalin's pragmatic and ruthless approach to governance is highlighted in this quote. His reign was marked by widespread purges, including the Great Purge of the 1930s, where millions were executed or sent to the Gulag labor camps. Stalin's policies and actions resulted in the deaths of millions, reflecting his willingness to use extreme measures to maintain control and achieve his goals.

> ### *"In the Soviet army, it takes more courage to retreat than advance."*

This quote from Stalin reflects his harsh military strategy during World War II. As the leader of the Soviet Union, he demanded absolute dedication and sacrifice from his troops. His policies included harsh penalties for desertion and retreat, exemplifying his belief in total commitment to the war effort. Stalin's leadership was crucial during key battles such as

Stalingrad, where Soviet forces ultimately turned the tide against the Nazis.

"Gratitude is a sickness suffered by dogs."

Stalin's dismissive view of loyalty and gratitude is evident in this quote. Despite his reliance on close associates to implement his policies, Stalin often treated them with suspicion and paranoia. Many of his trusted aides and military leaders were eventually purged or executed. Stalin's regime was characterized by a climate of fear and mistrust, where loyalty was often met with betrayal.

"I trust no one, not even myself."

This quote underscores Stalin's deep-seated paranoia and distrust. His suspicion extended to all levels of society, including his inner circle. Stalin's regime was marked by constant surveillance, espionage, and a pervasive security apparatus designed to root out perceived enemies. This atmosphere of fear ensured that dissent was swiftly and brutally suppressed.

"Education is a weapon whose effects depend on who holds it in his hands and at whom it is aimed."

Stalin recognized the power of education and propaganda in shaping the future of the Soviet Union. He implemented widespread educational reforms aimed at promoting communist ideology and loyalty to the state. Under Stalin, education became a tool for indoctrination, with a strong emphasis on

Marxist-Leninist principles and the glorification of Soviet achievements.

> ## *"History has shown there are no invincible armies."*

Stalin's recognition of the fluid nature of military power is reflected in this quote. His leadership during World War II involved significant strategic decisions, such as the relocation of industrial resources and the implementation of scorched earth policies. Stalin's understanding of the importance of adaptability and resilience contributed to the eventual Soviet victory over Nazi Germany.

> ## *"The death of one man is a tragedy, the death of millions is a statistic."*

This quote is often attributed to Stalin and reflects his utilitarian approach to governance. Stalin's policies, including forced collectivization and the Great Terror, led to widespread suffering and loss of life. His legacy is marked by the transformation of the Soviet Union into a major world power at the cost of immense human suffering and repression.

Did you know?

Before becoming the leader of the Soviet Union, Joseph Stalin was involved in bank robberies and other criminal activities to fund the Bolshevik movement. His involvement in the 1907 Tiflis bank robbery, which resulted in significant financial gains for the Bolsheviks, showcased his willingness to use any means necessary to support the revolutionary cause. This ruthless pragmatism would define his later leadership style.

Unlikely Allies: The Battle of Castle Itter

Amidst the chaos and conflict of World War II, there emerged an extraordinary and unlikely alliance at the Battle of Castle Itter. In this peculiar clash, American GIs and German Wehrmacht soldiers found themselves fighting side-by-side against the notorious Waffen-SS. This bizarre and unique engagement took place in a small Austrian castle, where both forces united to defend a group of high-profile prisoners, including two former French prime ministers, a famous tennis player, and General de Gaulle's sister.

By May 1945, the war in Europe was nearing its end. Nazi Germany was on the brink of collapse, and Allied forces were rapidly advancing across the continent. Castle Itter, located in the Austrian Alps, had been transformed into a prison by the Nazis to hold prominent French prisoners. As the war drew to a close, the castle became a focal point of a remarkable last stand involving unlikely allies against the desperate and fanatical SS troops.

The genesis of this unusual alliance began when Captain Jack Lee, an American tank commander, received a distress call about the castle. Simultaneously, Major Josef Gangl, a German Wehrmacht officer sympathetic to the anti-Nazi resistance, realized the danger posed by the approaching SS forces. Gangl and his men decided to surrender to the Americans, recognizing a mutual interest in saving the prisoners and protecting the castle.

On May 5, 1945, the combined force of American and German soldiers, along with the French prisoners, prepared to defend Castle Itter. The defenders included former French Prime Ministers Édouard Daladier and Paul Reynaud, famous tennis player Jean Borotra, and General de Gaulle's sister, among others. As the Waffen-SS launched their attack, the defenders braced themselves for a fierce battle. Despite their differences, the Americans and Germans worked together, manning machine guns and coordinating their defense strategy.

A Fierce Defense

The battle was intense, with the Waffen-SS determined to recapture the castle and eliminate the prisoners. Captain Lee and Major Gangl led their men with remarkable coordination and bravery. Jean Borotra, the tennis player, volunteered to leap over the castle walls to seek additional help, successfully bringing reinforcements from a nearby American unit. The defenders, though outnumbered, managed to hold their ground, utilizing the castle's strategic vantage points and fortifications.

The arrival of the reinforcements marked a turning point in the battle. The combined firepower and resolve of the defenders began to wear down the SS attackers. Major Gangl, despite his efforts, was tragically killed during the fighting. However, his sacrifice and the unwavering cooperation between the American and German soldiers led to the eventual defeat of the SS forces. By the end of the day, the castle and its prisoners were secured, marking a surreal victory achieved through an unprecedented alliance.

The Battle of Castle Itter stands as a unique footnote in the annals of World War II history. It exemplifies the complexities and strange bedfellows that war can create. This extraordinary event demonstrated that even in the darkest times, common humanity and shared goals could unite even the most unlikely of allies. The successful defense of the castle not only saved the lives of the prominent prisoners but also symbolized a rare moment of unity in a world torn apart by conflict.

The story of the Battle of Castle Itter is a powerful reminder of the unpredictable nature of war and the capacity for cooperation and bravery among soldiers. It challenges the conventional narratives of clear-cut enemy lines and highlights the nuanced realities of wartime alliances. As an emblem of resilience and unexpected camaraderie, the battle continues to fascinate and inspire, underscoring the enduring human spirit in the face of adversity.

- The Battle of Castle Itter is unique in World War II history as the only known instance where American and German soldiers fought side-by-side against a common enemy. This unprecedented collaboration occurred just days before the war in Europe ended, highlighting the chaotic and rapidly changing dynamics of the final days of the conflict.
- The French prisoners, who included high-ranking officials and prominent figures, did not remain passive during the battle. They took up arms alongside their rescuers, demonstrating remarkable bravery and resourcefulness. Jean Borotra, the famous tennis player, notably volunteered to jump over the castle walls to summon additional help from American forces.
- Major Josef Gangl, a Wehrmacht officer, had been secretly working with the Austrian resistance against the Nazis even before the battle. His decision to collaborate with the Americans and defend the castle was a continuation of his efforts to undermine the Nazi regime. Gangl's actions during the battle cemented his legacy as a hero of the resistance.
- Castle Itter, located in the Tyrol region of Austria, was strategically important due to its position and its use as a prison for high-profile French prisoners. Its defense was crucial not only for saving the lives of the prisoners but also for preventing the SS from using the location as a stronghold in the final days of the war.
- Members of the Austrian resistance played a critical role in the defense of Castle Itter. They provided intelligence, logistical support, and additional manpower to the defenders. The collaboration between American soldiers, Wehrmacht defectors, and the Austrian resistance showcased a united front against the SS, contributing significantly to the successful defense of the castle.

Nuremberg Trials Fact File

Historic Judicial Precedent: The Nuremberg Trials were the first trials of their kind, establishing a precedent for international law by holding individuals, including heads of state, accountable for war crimes, crimes against humanity, and genocide. They set the foundation for modern international criminal law and the establishment of future international tribunals.

Initiated by Allied Powers: The trials were initiated by the Allied powers—United States, Soviet Union, United Kingdom, and France—following the defeat of Nazi Germany. They aimed to bring Nazi war criminals to justice and were held in Nuremberg, Germany, chosen for its symbolic value as a former Nazi rallying site.

IMT and Subsequent Trials: The Nuremberg Trials consisted of two sets of proceedings: the International Military Tribunal (IMT), which tried the major war criminals from November 20, 1945, to October 1, 1946, and the subsequent Nuremberg Military Tribunals (NMT), which tried lower-ranking officials, industrialists, and military leaders from 1946 to 1949.

Indictment Categories: The IMT focused on four major categories of charges: crimes against peace (planning and initiating war), war crimes (violations of the laws of war), crimes against humanity (atrocities against civilians, including genocide), and conspiracy to commit these crimes.

High-Profile Defendants: Notable defendants included Hermann Göring, Rudolf Hess, Joachim von Ribbentrop, Wilhelm Keitel, and Albert Speer. Of the 24 principal defendants in the IMT, 12 were sentenced to death, three were acquitted, and the rest received various prison sentences.

Justice Robert H. Jackson: U.S. Supreme Court Justice Robert H. Jackson served as the chief prosecutor for the United States. His opening and closing statements eloquently articulated the moral and legal imperatives of the trials, emphasizing the pursuit of justice over vengeance.

Documentation and Evidence: The trials relied heavily on documentary evidence, including official Nazi records, orders, and photographs, as well as testimonies from survivors and eyewitnesses. This methodical approach helped establish a comprehensive historical record of Nazi atrocities.

Legal Innovations: The trials introduced several legal innovations, including the concept of individual accountability for war crimes and the rejection of "just following orders" as a valid defense. These principles have since been integrated into international law.

Legacy and Influence: The Nuremberg Trials influenced the development of subsequent international legal frameworks, including the Genocide Convention (1948), the Universal Declaration of Human Rights (1948), and the establishment of the International Criminal Court (ICC) in 2002.

Criticisms and Controversies: Despite their groundbreaking nature, the trials faced criticisms, including allegations of "victor's justice" and questions about the fairness of prosecuting individuals for actions that were not clearly defined as crimes under international law at the time they were committed. Nonetheless, they remain a landmark in the pursuit of justice and accountability for war crimes.

Fire from the Sky: Japan's Failed Incendiary Balloon Campaign

During World War II, the Japanese military devised an ambitious and unconventional strategy to attack the United States directly. This strategy involved launching thousands of high-altitude incendiary balloons across the Pacific Ocean, aimed at starting forest fires in the American Northwest. These balloons, known as Fu-Go, represented an innovative yet ultimately unsuccessful attempt to cause widespread destruction and panic on American soil.

In late 1944, as the war increasingly turned against Japan, Japanese military planners sought new ways to strike at the United States. Traditional military engagements were proving less effective, and Japan was eager to find methods that could bypass America's formidable defenses. The idea of using the jet stream to carry incendiary balloons across the Pacific was both daring and technically challenging. The balloons were designed to carry incendiary devices that would ignite upon landing, ideally setting vast tracts of forest ablaze.

The Fu-Go Balloons

Over 9,000 Fu-Go balloons were launched from various sites in Japan between November 1944 and April 1945.

These balloons were made from lightweight paper and rubberized silk, filled with hydrogen, and equipped with sophisticated altitude control mechanisms to keep them within the jet stream. Each balloon carried several incendiary devices and occasionally anti-personnel bombs, intended to ignite fires upon landing in the forests of the Pacific Northwest.

Despite the technical ingenuity behind the Fu-Go balloons, their impact was minimal. Most of the balloons either fell into the ocean or landed in remote areas without causing significant damage. The few that did reach the mainland were largely ineffective due to the damp conditions of the forests they landed in. The wet and snowy winter of 1944-1945 further reduced the likelihood of large-scale forest fires. Only a handful of minor fires were reported, all of which were quickly contained without significant damage.

The Fu-Go campaign is remembered primarily for one tragic incident. On May 5, 1945, a balloon bomb explosion killed six civilians near Bly, Oregon. A woman and five children, who were on a church picnic, discovered the unexploded device and accidentally triggered it. This incident remains the only instance of fatalities on the continental United States as a direct result of enemy action during World War II. It highlighted the potential danger of the balloon bombs, even though the campaign failed to achieve its broader objectives.

The Fu-Go balloon campaign, while innovative, ultimately failed to achieve its strategic goals. The balloons were largely ineffective in causing the widespread destruction Japan had hoped for, and their impact on the American war effort was negligible. However, the campaign serves as a fascinating example of the lengths to which wartime innovation can go, illustrating both the ingenuity and desperation of the Japanese military in the closing stages of the war. Today, the story of the Fu-Go balloons stands as a unique chapter in the history of World War II, reminding us of the diverse and sometimes unexpected tactics employed during the conflict.

- Approximately 300 of the 9,000 launched Fu-Go balloons are believed to have reached the continental United States, with sightings reported from Alaska to Mexico and as far east as Michigan.
- The balloons were equipped with a barometric pressure switch that triggered the release of ballast sandbags to maintain altitude. This sophisticated mechanism allowed the balloons to stay within the high-altitude jet stream across the Pacific.
- Unexploded balloon bombs continued to be found for years after the war. The last known incident occurred in 1955 when a bomb was discovered in Alaska. Authorities continue to warn that some unexploded devices might still be hidden in remote areas.

The Code Talkers: Native American Linguists of World War II

In the heart of the Pacific campaign during World War II, the United States military employed an ingenious and secretive method of communication that significantly contributed to their success: the use of Native American languages to transmit top-secret messages. Among the most renowned were the Navajo Code Talkers, whose unique linguistic abilities provided an unbreakable code that baffled Japanese intelligence and played a crucial role in the Allied victory.

The concept of using Native American languages for secure communications arose from the need for a code that could not be easily deciphered by enemy forces. The Navajo language was chosen due to its complexity and obscurity; it was an unwritten language known to very few outside the Navajo community. Furthermore, it had no similarities to Japanese, making it an ideal choice for secure military communications.

The Navajo Code Talkers program was initiated in 1942 when Philip Johnston, a World War I veteran who had grown up on a Navajo reservation, proposed the idea to the U.S. Marine Corps. Johnston knew that Navajo, with its unique syntax and phonology, would be nearly impossible for non-speakers to learn and decode. The Marines enlisted 29 Navajo men, who developed a complex code based on their language, using Navajo words to represent military terms and the phonetic alphabet.

The Navajo Code Talkers developed a two-part code system. The first part involved using Navajo words to represent letters of the English alphabet, allowing them to spell out words. For example, "wol-la-chee" (ant) represented "A," and "shush" (bear) represented "B." The second part of the code used Navajo words to substitute for entire military terms, making it even more secure. For instance, "besh-lo" (iron fish) meant "submarine." This layered approach ensured that even if an enemy intercepted the message, it would be almost impossible to understand.

The Navajo Code Talkers played a crucial role in several key battles in the Pacific, including Guadalcanal, Iwo Jima, and Okinawa. Their ability to quickly and accurately transmit messages under fire saved countless lives and ensured the success of many operations. The Japanese, skilled codebreakers themselves, never succeeded in cracking the Navajo code, which remained unbroken throughout the war.

The contributions of the Navajo Code Talkers went unrecognized for many years due to the classified nature of their work. It wasn't until 1968 that their role was declassified, and they began to receive the recognition they deserved. In 2001, President George W. Bush awarded the original 29 Code Talkers the Congressional Gold Medal, with subsequent Code Talkers receiving the Silver Medal. Their legacy lives on as a testament to their bravery, skill, and unique contribution to the war effort.

The story of the Navajo Code Talkers is a remarkable example of how linguistic diversity and cultural heritage can be leveraged in innovative ways during times of conflict. Their unbreakable code provided the U.S. military with a significant advantage in the Pacific Theater, demonstrating the crucial role of secure communications in modern warfare. The Navajo Code Talkers not only contributed to the Allied victory but also left an enduring legacy of courage and ingenuity.

Other Encryption Methods Used During World War II

Enigma Machine:

- The Enigma machine was a cipher device used by Nazi Germany, known for its complex encryption capabilities. It required the precise alignment of rotors and settings to decode messages. The efforts of Allied cryptanalysts, particularly at Bletchley Park, led to the eventual cracking of Enigma, significantly aiding the war effort.

Purple Machine:

- The Purple machine was a Japanese cipher device used to encrypt diplomatic messages. American cryptanalysts, including those at the Signal Intelligence Service, managed to break the Purple code, providing crucial intelligence about Japanese plans and strategies.

SIGABA:

- SIGABA, also known as ECM Mark II, was an American cipher machine used by the U.S. during World War II. It was considered more secure than the Enigma machine and was never known to be cracked by

Axis forces. It was used for high-level communications between Allied commanders.

Lorenz Cipher:

- The Lorenz cipher was used by the German High Command to encrypt messages between Hitler and his generals. It was more complex than Enigma, using 12 rotors for encryption. British cryptanalysts, including those at Bletchley Park, developed techniques to intercept and decrypt Lorenz-encrypted messages, providing valuable strategic information.

Typex:

- The Typex machine was a British cipher device based on the Enigma design but with additional security features. It was used by the British armed forces and proved effective in securing Allied communications, contributing to the overall success of the Allied encryption efforts during the war.

Wartime Japan Quiz

1. Which 1931 event marked the beginning of Japan's aggressive expansion in Asia?

    a) Manchurian Incident
    b) Marco Polo Bridge Incident
    c) Attack on Pearl Harbor

2. What was the name of Japan's military strategy aiming for quick victories and expansion across Asia and the Pacific?

    a) Blitzkrieg
    b) Greater East Asia Co-Prosperity Sphere
    c) Bushido Code

3. Who was the Prime Minister of Japan during most of World War II?

    a) Hirohito
    b) Hideki Tojo
    c) Isoroku Yamamoto

4. Which city suffered the first atomic bombing in history?

    a) Tokyo
    b) Hiroshima
    c) Nagasaki

5. What was the name of the Japanese suicide pilots who attacked Allied ships?

    a) Samurai
    b) Shogun
    c) Kamikaze

6. What was the infamous march where thousands of American and Filipino prisoners of war died in the Philippines?

    a) Death March of Manila

- b) Bataan Death March
- c) Leyte Gulf March

7. Which 1942 battle was a turning point in the Pacific War, halting Japanese expansion?

- a) Battle of Midway
- b) Battle of the Coral Sea
- c) Battle of Okinawa

8. What was Japan's code of honor and discipline for its soldiers, emphasizing loyalty and sacrifice?

- a) Seppuku
- b) Samurai Code
- c) Bushido

9. Which 1937 atrocity involved mass killings and rapes committed by Japanese soldiers in China?

- a) Rape of Nanking
- b) Shanghai Massacre
- c) Beijing Atrocity

10. What was the Japanese strategy of building heavily fortified island bases to defend against Allied advances?

- a) Island Hopping
- b) Fortress Islands
- c) Defensive Perimeter Strategy

Answers

1. a) Manchurian Incident

- The Manchurian Incident, also known as the Mukden Incident, occurred on September 18, 1931, and marked the beginning of Japan's aggressive expansion. Japanese troops used a staged explosion as a pretext to invade and occupy Manchuria, setting up the puppet state of Manchukuo.

2. b) Greater East Asia Co-Prosperity Sphere

- The Greater East Asia Co-Prosperity Sphere was Japan's strategy aiming for quick victories and expansion across Asia and the Pacific. It was promoted as a way to liberate Asian countries from Western colonial rule but was actually intended to establish Japanese dominance in the region.

3. b) Hideki Tojo

- Hideki Tojo served as Prime Minister of Japan during most of World War II, from 1941 to 1944. He was a leading advocate for Japan's military expansion and played a central role in the decision to attack Pearl Harbor.

4. b) Hiroshima

- Hiroshima was the first city to suffer an atomic bombing, on August 6, 1945. The bombing, conducted by the United States, resulted in massive destruction and significant loss of life, contributing to Japan's eventual surrender.

5. c) Kamikaze

- Kamikaze pilots were Japanese suicide pilots who deliberately crashed their aircraft into Allied ships during World War II. The term "kamikaze" means "divine wind," and these pilots were seen as making the ultimate sacrifice for their country.

6. b) Bataan Death March

- The Bataan Death March occurred in April 1942, when Japanese forces forcibly transferred American and Filipino prisoners of war from Bataan to prison camps. Thousands died from brutality, starvation, and disease during the march.

7. a) Battle of Midway

- The Battle of Midway, fought in June 1942, was a turning point in the Pacific War. The United States Navy's decisive victory over the Japanese fleet halted Japan's expansion and began a series of Allied offensives that eventually led to Japan's defeat.

8. c) Bushido

- Bushido, meaning "the way of the warrior," was Japan's code of honor and discipline for its soldiers. It emphasized loyalty, honor, and sacrifice, guiding the conduct of Japanese military personnel during the war.

9. a) Rape of Nanking

- The Rape of Nanking, also known as the Nanking Massacre, took place in December 1937 when Japanese troops captured Nanking (Nanjing), the capital of China. The atrocity involved mass killings, rapes, and looting, resulting in the deaths of hundreds of thousands of Chinese civilians and disarmed soldiers.

10. c) Defensive Perimeter Strategy

- The Defensive Perimeter Strategy involved building heavily fortified island bases across the Pacific to defend against Allied advances. These fortifications were intended to create a strong defensive network, making it difficult for the Allies to penetrate Japanese-held territories.

Father of the Atomic Bomb

J. Robert Oppenheimer, often referred to as the "father of the atomic bomb," played a pivotal role in the development of nuclear weapons during World War II. Born on April 22, 1904, Oppenheimer was a brilliant physicist whose leadership of the Manhattan Project significantly altered the course of history. The project, a top-secret initiative, was launched in 1942 to develop an atomic bomb before Nazi Germany could achieve the same goal. Oppenheimer was appointed as the scientific director of the project and led a team of some of the greatest scientific minds of the time at Los Alamos Laboratory in New Mexico.

Under Oppenheimer's guidance, the team made rapid progress, culminating in the successful detonation of the first atomic bomb, code-named "Trinity," on July 16, 1945, in the New Mexico desert. This test marked the first instance of a nuclear explosion and demonstrated the bomb's devastating power. Following the Trinity test, Oppenheimer famously quoted the Bhagavad Gita, reflecting on the profound implications of their achievement: "Now I am become Death, the destroyer of worlds."

The success of the Manhattan Project led to the deployment of atomic bombs on Hiroshima and Nagasaki in August 1945, which played a critical role in bringing World War II to an end. Despite the scientific triumph, Oppenheimer grappled with the ethical and moral ramifications of the atomic bomb's destructive capability. After the war, he became a prominent advocate for the control of nuclear weapons and international arms regulation, warning of the potential consequences of a nuclear arms race.

Oppenheimer's legacy is a complex blend of scientific achievement and ethical contemplation, highlighting the dual-edged nature of technological advancements.

His contributions to the development of nuclear physics and his subsequent efforts to promote peace and prevent nuclear proliferation remain significant in the annals of history.

Code Name "Trinity"

The name for the first atomic bomb test, "Trinity," was inspired by John Donne's poetry, reflecting Oppenheimer's love for literature and poetry.

Security Concerns

Despite his critical role, Oppenheimer's past associations with communist organizations led to intense scrutiny and a controversial security hearing in 1954, which resulted in the revocation of his security clearance.

Physicist's Dilemma

Oppenheimer was known for his complex personality, often described as both charming and enigmatic. He reportedly had a habit of greeting visitors to Los Alamos with the unsettling question, "Are you secure?"

Luxury Car

Oppenheimer drove a Cadillac, a luxury car, which was unusual for a scientist at the time, highlighting his unique blend of intellectual prowess and personal style.

Smoking Habit

Oppenheimer was a heavy smoker, often seen with a cigarette in hand, which contributed to his health issues later in life, including throat cancer.

Quantum Mechanics

Influence His interest in Eastern philosophy and the Bhagavad Gita influenced his perspective on quantum mechanics, blending scientific inquiry with philosophical thought.

Scientific Polymath

In addition to his work on the atomic bomb, Oppenheimer made significant contributions to astrophysics, quantum field theory, and the theory of black holes.

Code of Secrecy

The strict secrecy of the Manhattan Project meant that even Oppenheimer's mail was censored, and he had limited contact with the outside world during the project's peak.

Academic Legacy

Oppenheimer played a key role in founding the Institute for Advanced Study in Princeton, which became a leading center for theoretical research in physics and mathematics.

The Nazis' Sun Gun: A Sci-Fi Dream of Destruction

During World War II, the Nazi regime explored numerous advanced and often outlandish technologies in their quest for military superiority. Among the most ambitious was the concept of a 'sun gun,' a giant mirror placed in space designed to focus the sun's rays onto enemy cities, effectively turning them into fiery infernos. This fantastical idea was born out of a desire to harness futuristic technology for ultimate destructive power.

The sun gun concept was developed by German physicist Hermann Oberth, a pioneer in rocket science and space exploration. The idea involved launching a massive, mile-wide concave mirror into orbit, where it would concentrate sunlight onto a small area on Earth's surface. This concentrated beam of solar energy was intended to create intense heat, capable of igniting fires and causing widespread devastation. Although theoretically intriguing, the practical challenges of constructing and deploying such a device were insurmountable given the technology of the time.

Several significant obstacles made the sun gun project impractical. First, the sheer size and weight of the mirror would have required a launch vehicle far beyond the capabilities of World War II-era rocket technology. Additionally, maintaining the mirror's precise orientation and position in orbit to accurately target specific locations on Earth posed significant engineering challenges. The Nazis also lacked the materials and manufacturing techniques needed to create a mirror of the necessary scale and reflectivity.

As the war progressed and Germany faced increasing military pressure from the Allies, the focus shifted from speculative projects like the sun gun to more immediate and achievable technological advancements. The sun gun concept was ultimately dismissed as impossible with the existing technology, and resources were redirected to more practical weapons and defenses. The idea of using a giant space mirror to wreak havoc on enemy cities remained a science fiction fantasy, beyond the reach of 1940s engineering.

Other Inventions the Nazis Tried

1. V-2 Rockets:

- The V-2 rocket was the world's first long-range guided ballistic missile, developed by the Nazis and used against Allied cities. It represented a significant technological advancement in rocket science and laid the groundwork for post-war space exploration and missile technology.

2. Horten Ho 229:

- The Horten Ho 229 was an experimental jet-powered flying wing aircraft, considered a precursor to modern stealth technology. Its unique design aimed to reduce radar detection, though it never saw combat before the war ended.

3. Schwerer Gustav:

- Schwerer Gustav was a massive railway gun designed to destroy heavily fortified targets. Weighing nearly 1,350 tons and capable of firing shells over 40 kilometers, it was the largest caliber rifled weapon ever used in combat, though its effectiveness was limited by its cumbersome size.

4. Jet-Powered Aircraft:

- The Messerschmitt Me 262 was the world's first operational jet-powered fighter aircraft. Its advanced speed and firepower gave it a significant edge over Allied propeller-driven planes, but its impact was limited by production delays and fuel shortages.

Project Habakkuk: Britain's Icy Ambition

During World War II, the British military conceived a bold and unconventional plan to counter the threat of German U-boats in the Atlantic. This ambitious idea, known as Project Habakkuk, aimed to build a massive aircraft carrier out of pykrete, a remarkable mixture of ice and wood pulp. The project promised to revolutionize naval warfare by providing an unsinkable platform for aircraft in the mid-Atlantic, but it ultimately faced insurmountable challenges.

The brainchild of Geoffrey Pyke, a British inventor and military strategist, Project Habakkuk emerged from the urgent need to protect Allied shipping from relentless U-boat attacks. Pykrete, a material composed of 14% wood pulp and 86% ice, was discovered to be incredibly strong and resistant to melting. The plan was to construct a gigantic aircraft carrier using this material, which would serve as a floating airbase in the mid-Atlantic, beyond the range of land-based aircraft.

Engineering the Ice Carrier

The envisioned carrier was to be over 2,000 feet long and 300 feet wide, with a displacement of 2 million tons. It would house numerous aircraft and provide a strategic base for anti-submarine operations. Pykrete's unique properties made it an ideal candidate for this colossal structure; it was durable, self-sealing when damaged, and required minimal refrigeration to maintain. The project received support from notable figures, including Lord

Mountbatten and Prime Minister Winston Churchill, who were intrigued by its potential.

Despite initial enthusiasm, Project Habakkuk faced significant technical and logistical challenges. Constructing such a massive structure required an unprecedented amount of resources and labor. The logistics of building and maintaining the carrier in the harsh conditions of the Atlantic posed additional difficulties. Rising costs and the allocation of resources to more immediate wartime needs further complicated the project's feasibility.

As the war progressed, advancements in long-range aircraft and improved convoy escorts reduced the strategic necessity of a mid-Atlantic aircraft carrier. The introduction of long-range bombers and escort carriers made it possible to provide air cover for convoys across the entire Atlantic, diminishing the need for Project Habakkuk. Additionally, the estimated costs of constructing and maintaining the ice carrier continued to escalate, making the project increasingly untenable.

By 1943, Project Habakkuk was officially abandoned. While it never materialized, the project remains a fascinating example of wartime innovation and the lengths to which the Allies were willing to go to gain an edge over their enemies. The concept of using pykrete for large-scale structures demonstrated remarkable creativity and highlighted the inventive spirit that characterized many wartime efforts.

1. Bouncing Bombs:
- Developed by Barnes Wallis, these bombs were designed to skip over water and explode against the dams of the Ruhr Valley. The successful "Dambusters" raid in 1943 caused significant flooding and disrupted German industry.

2. Hedgehog Anti-Submarine Weapon:

- A forward-throwing anti-submarine weapon that fired a salvo of small bombs ahead of a ship. It increased the chances of hitting a submerged submarine and became a standard anti-submarine weapon for the Allies.

3. Mulberry Harbors:

- Portable, temporary harbors constructed by the Allies to facilitate rapid offloading of cargo onto the beaches during the Normandy invasion. These artificial harbors were crucial in supporting the D-Day landings and subsequent operations in France.

4. Pluto (Pipeline Under the Ocean):

- An undersea pipeline system developed to transport fuel from England to the Allied forces in Normandy. It provided a reliable supply of fuel crucial for the success of the Allied advance following the D-Day landings.

5. Oboe Navigation System:

- A radio navigation system used by the Royal Air Force to improve bombing accuracy. It guided bombers to their targets with greater precision, enhancing the effectiveness of bombing raids against German industrial and military installations.

Lady Death: The Fearsome Sniper of the Soviet Union

In the annals of World War II, few stories are as remarkable and awe-inspiring as that of Lyudmila Pavlichenko, the Soviet sniper famously known as "Lady Death." Her extraordinary marksmanship and lethal efficiency on the battlefield earned her a place among the deadliest snipers in history. With 309 confirmed kills to her name, Pavlichenko's legacy is one of unparalleled skill and unwavering courage in the face of the enemy.

Lyudmila Pavlichenko was born in 1916 in Bila Tserkva, Ukraine. From a young age, she exhibited a strong will and a competitive spirit, which she later channeled into her training as a sniper. When Nazi Germany invaded the Soviet Union in 1941, Pavlichenko was among the first women to volunteer for combat. She quickly proved her prowess with a rifle, and her reputation as a deadly sniper began to grow.

Pavlichenko's first major engagement was during the defense of Odessa, where she made her mark with an impressive number of kills. Her skills were further honed during the prolonged siege of Sevastopol on the Crimean Peninsula. Her confirmed kill count of 309 enemy soldiers, including 36 enemy snipers, placed her among the top snipers of the war. Despite being injured by mortar fire, she continued to fight until she was finally evacuated to Moscow for recovery.

Despite the dangers and the physical and emotional toll of combat, Pavlichenko remained resolute. Her remarkable achievements on the battlefield made her a national hero and a symbol of Soviet resilience and determination. Her kill count is believed to be even higher than the confirmed 309, underscoring her effectiveness and fearlessness as a sniper.

A Diplomatic Warrior

After being evacuated due to her injuries, Pavlichenko was sent on a goodwill tour to the United States and Canada. She became the first Soviet citizen to be received at the White House by President Franklin D. Roosevelt. Her tour was aimed at garnering support for the Soviet war effort, and she impressed audiences with her poise and powerful speeches. Despite the horrors she had witnessed, Pavlichenko continued to advocate for her country and its fight against fascism.

1. Vasily Zaytsev:
- Another legendary Soviet sniper, Zaytsev is best known for his role in the Battle of Stalingrad, where he killed 225 enemy soldiers and became a symbol of Soviet resistance.

2. Mariya Vasilyevna Oktyabrskaya:
- After her husband was killed in battle, Oktyabrskaya sold her possessions to fund a tank, which she then drove into combat herself. She named the tank "Fighting Girlfriend" and became a decorated tank driver and mechanic.

3. Nina Petrova:
- A senior sniper, Petrova was one of the oldest female snipers in the Soviet army, credited with 122 confirmed kills and awarded numerous medals for her bravery and skill.

4. Ivan Sidorenko:
- Sidorenko was one of the Soviet Union's top snipers, with over 500 confirmed kills. He also trained other snipers, significantly contributing to the Soviet sniper program.

5. Lyudmila Mikhailovna Pavlichenko:
- Not to be confused with Lady Death, this Lyudmila was another accomplished sniper with numerous confirmed kills, highlighting the prominence of female snipers in the Soviet military.

6. Roza Shanina:

- A sniper credited with 59 confirmed kills, Shanina was known for her exceptional marksmanship and bravery, often volunteering for dangerous missions.

7. Aleksandra Samusenko:

- A tank commander, Samusenko was one of the few female tank commanders in the Soviet army, known for her leadership and bravery in battle.

8. Yevdokiya Zavaly:

- The only female commander of a platoon of marines in the Soviet Union, Zavaly fought in numerous key battles and was known for her fearlessness and tactical acumen.

9. Manshuk Mametova:

- A machine gunner who displayed extraordinary courage, Mametova was posthumously awarded the title Hero of the Soviet Union for her actions in battle.

10. Yekaterina Budanova:

- One of the few female fighter pilots, Budanova was credited with 11 solo victories and 3 shared kills, becoming one of the top female aces of the war.

The story of Lyudmila Pavlichenko, along with the remarkable tales of other Soviet fighters, showcases the incredible bravery, skill, and resilience of those who fought against the Axis powers. These individuals, many of whom overcame significant personal challenges, played crucial roles in the Soviet Union's war effort and left indelible marks on history. Their legacies continue to inspire and remind us of the extraordinary contributions made by women and men alike in times of conflict.

Pearl Harbor Attack

On December 7, 1941, the Japanese Imperial Navy launched a surprise military strike against the United States naval base at Pearl Harbor, Hawaii. This meticulously planned attack aimed to cripple the U.S. Pacific Fleet, thereby preventing American interference in Japan's expansionist activities in Southeast Asia. The assault began at 7:48 a.m. Hawaiian Time, involving over 350 aircraft, including bombers, fighters, and torpedo planes. The attack was devastating, resulting in the sinking or damaging of eight battleships, including the USS Arizona and USS Oklahoma, as well as numerous cruisers, destroyers, and other vessels. Over 180 U.S. aircraft were destroyed, and more than 2,400 Americans lost their lives, with another 1,000 wounded. The sheer scale and surprise of the attack stunned the American public and military alike.

In the aftermath, President Franklin D. Roosevelt addressed the nation, famously describing December 7th as "a date which will live in infamy." The attack galvanized the United States, leading to a swift declaration of war against Japan on December 8, 1941. This declaration brought the U.S. into World War II, significantly altering the course of the conflict. The attack on Pearl Harbor united the American people, previously divided on the issue of entering the war, and marked the beginning of a significant American military and industrial mobilization effort. This turning point also set the stage for the broader Pacific Theater operations, where the United States would eventually gain the upper hand against Japanese forces.

- There has been considerable debate over whether U.S. intelligence had advance warnings of the attack. While there were indications of increased Japanese activity, the precise time and location of the attack were not anticipated.
- In addition to aircraft, Japan used midget submarines to infiltrate the harbor. Five midget submarines were involved, but they were largely ineffective, with one being captured and others sunk.

- U.S. code breakers had deciphered Japanese communications indicating a potential threat, but misinterpretations and delays in communication meant that the warnings were not acted upon in time.
- The USS Arizona remains sunken in Pearl Harbor, serving as a memorial to those who lost their lives. The site is a poignant reminder of the attack and is visited by millions annually.
- Within hours of the attack, the United States began mobilizing its military forces, and many young Americans volunteered for service, marking a significant shift in national sentiment toward the war.
- The attack led to a massive increase in U.S. military production and economic activity, significantly boosting the American economy and ending the Great Depression era's high unemployment rates.
- Although the attack was tactically successful, it strategically backfired by bringing the U.S., with its vast industrial and military capacity, fully into the war, ultimately contributing to Japan's defeat.
- A planned third wave of attacks, targeting fuel storage tanks and repair facilities, was called off by the Japanese commander, Admiral Nagumo, a decision that allowed the U.S. Navy to recover more rapidly than anticipated.
- The attack worsened relations between the U.S. and its Japanese-American citizens, leading to the internment of over 120,000 Japanese-Americans.

"Yesterday, December 7, 1941—a date which will live in infamy—the United States of America was suddenly and deliberately attacked by naval and air forces of the Empire of Japan." — President Franklin D. Roosevelt

The Ghost Army: America's Masters of Deception

During World War II, the United States deployed a unique and highly secretive unit known as the 'Ghost Army.' This extraordinary group of 1,100 men had a singular mission: to deceive the German military about the location, strength, and intentions of Allied forces. Through elaborate and innovative methods, the Ghost Army carried out over 20 successful deceptions, playing a crucial role in the Allied war effort.

The Ghost Army, officially known as the 23rd Headquarters Special Troops, was established in 1944. The unit was composed of artists, actors, sound engineers, and other creative professionals who were tasked with using their skills to craft elaborate deceptions. Their operations were designed to mislead the German military, diverting attention and resources away from real Allied movements and objectives.

Ingenious Tactics

The Ghost Army employed a variety of ingenious tactics to achieve their goals. One of their primary methods was the use of inflatable tanks, planes, and artillery. These life-sized rubber decoys were strategically placed in fields to create the illusion of a large military presence. From a distance, these inflatable models were indistinguishable from the real thing, fooling enemy reconnaissance.

In addition to visual deceptions, the Ghost Army utilized auditory tricks. They created fake radio transmissions to simulate troop movements and communications. Skilled actors impersonated high-ranking officers, giving orders and discussing plans that were entirely fictitious. These radio broadcasts were carefully crafted to match the style and content of genuine military communications, further enhancing the credibility of the ruse.

One of the Ghost Army's most significant operations took place during the Battle of the Bulge. In December 1944, as the German forces launched a surprise counteroffensive, the Ghost Army set up a phony headquarters and generated fake radio traffic to suggest that the Allies were preparing a major counterattack. This deception helped to confuse the German command and contributed to the eventual Allied victory.

Another notable operation occurred in the lead-up to the D-Day invasion. The Ghost Army played a crucial role in Operation Fortitude, the broader deception plan designed to mislead the Germans about the true landing site. By creating the illusion of a large force preparing to invade Pas-de-Calais, they diverted German attention and reinforcements away from Normandy, aiding the success of the actual landings.

The efforts of the Ghost Army had a profound impact on the war. Their deceptions sowed confusion and uncertainty within the German high command, leading to strategic miscalculations and the misallocation of resources. By successfully misleading the enemy, the Ghost Army helped to protect Allied troops and facilitate key operations, contributing significantly to the overall success of the Allied campaign in Europe.

For many years, the activities of the Ghost Army remained classified, and their contributions went largely unrecognized. However, in recent years, their story has come to light, highlighting the incredible ingenuity and creativity of these unsung heroes. The Ghost Army's legacy is a testament to the power of deception and the vital role that unconventional tactics can play in warfare.

The Ghost Army's story is a remarkable chapter in the history of World War II, showcasing the innovative and resourceful methods employed by the Allies to secure victory. Through their imaginative deceptions, these 1,100 men not only misled the enemy but also protected countless lives and facilitated crucial military operations. Their legacy continues to inspire and reminds us of the diverse and ingenious strategies that can turn the tide of war.

1. Operation Fortitude:

- This larger deception plan, which included the Ghost Army, was designed to convince the Germans that the Allied invasion would occur at Pas-de-Calais rather than Normandy. It involved fake radio traffic, double agents, and the creation of phantom armies to mislead the enemy.

2. Operation Bodyguard:

- A strategic deception plan aimed at misleading the Axis powers about the timing and location of the Allied invasions of Europe. It included multiple subsidiary operations, such as Fortitude, and played a key role in the success of D-Day.

3. Operation Mincemeat:

- A British deception operation that involved planting false documents on a dead body, which was then allowed to wash ashore in Spain. The documents misled the Germans into believing that the Allies would invade Greece and Sardinia, rather than Sicily, facilitating a successful invasion of Sicily.

4. Double Cross System:

- A British intelligence operation that turned German spies in Britain into double agents. These agents were used to feed false information to the Germans, playing a crucial role in deceiving the enemy about Allied plans and movements.

5. Dummy Paratroopers (Rupert Dolls):

- During the D-Day invasion, the Allies dropped thousands of dummy paratroopers, known as Rupert dolls, to create the illusion of a large airborne assault. These dummies were equipped with recordings of gunfire and exploding firecrackers to further convince the Germans of a major paratrooper landing.

The Hidden Cave of Gibraltar: The Royal Navy's Secret Operations Centre

During World War II, the strategic importance of Gibraltar, a British Overseas Territory located at the entrance of the Mediterranean, was undeniable. The Royal Navy, ever vigilant and resourceful, devised an extraordinary plan to maintain surveillance over Axis operations in the area should Gibraltar fall into enemy hands. This plan involved creating a secret operations centre inside a cave, where six men would be sealed in to continue monitoring and reporting on enemy movements. Although the plan was eventually abandoned, the hidden cave was only discovered in 1997, revealing one of the war's most fascinating secrets.

The idea behind the secret operations centre was both simple and audacious. If the Nazis managed to capture Gibraltar, a team of six men would be sealed inside a specially prepared cave. Equipped with supplies and communication equipment, these men would conduct clandestine surveillance and report on Axis activities. The cave was outfitted with everything necessary for the men to survive and operate undetected for an extended period.

Preparation and Execution

The cave, known as Operation Tracer, was meticulously prepared. It included living quarters, a communications room, and an observation post with a view over the Mediterranean. The selected personnel underwent rigorous training and were ready to be sealed inside the cave at a moment's notice. The plan demonstrated the Royal Navy's commitment to maintaining a strategic advantage, even in the most adverse circumstances.

As the war progressed and the threat of Gibraltar being captured diminished, the plan was ultimately scrapped. The cave was sealed up and its existence forgotten. It wasn't until 1997, during an exploration by the Gibraltar Caving Group, that the hidden operations centre was rediscovered. The discovery provided a remarkable glimpse into the lengths the Royal Navy was willing to go to ensure continued intelligence gathering and strategic advantage.

The story of the hidden cave in Gibraltar is a testament to the ingenuity and determination of the Royal Navy during World War II. It highlights the importance placed on intelligence and the creative solutions developed to maintain it. While the plan was never put into action, the preparation and secrecy surrounding Operation Tracer remain a fascinating chapter in wartime history.

- During World War II, the British considered building massive aircraft carriers out of pykrete, a mixture of ice and wood pulp. The idea was to create unsinkable floating platforms in the Atlantic Ocean. Although the plan was eventually deemed impractical, small-scale prototypes were tested in Canada.

- During the Vietnam War, the U.S. Navy conducted weather modification operations under Operation Popeye. The goal was to extend the monsoon season over the Ho Chi Minh Trail by seeding clouds to induce rain, thereby disrupting enemy supply lines. The operation was classified for many years and remains one of the most unusual uses of weather manipulation in warfare.

- In World War I and World War II, the Royal Navy used "dazzle camouflage" on their ships. This technique involved painting ships in complex patterns of geometric shapes and contrasting colors. Rather than hiding the ships, the purpose was to confuse enemy rangefinders and make it difficult to estimate the ships' speed and direction.

- The U.S. Navy's NR-1 was a unique nuclear-powered submarine designed for underwater research and surveillance. Launched in 1969, it could stay submerged for extended periods and was used for secret missions, including recovering lost weapons and conducting espionage. It featured wheels for crawling along the ocean floor and had a small crew.

- During World War II, the Royal Navy and the United States conducted experiments to create a "tsunami bomb" under Project Seal. The idea was to use underwater explosions to generate tsunamis capable of devastating coastal cities. While tests showed some potential, the project was never fully developed or used in combat.

Operation Tannenbaum: Hitler's Unseen Plan to Invade Switzerland

Amidst the widespread devastation and conquest that marked Nazi Germany's rampage through Europe, one country managed to maintain its neutrality: Switzerland. Known for its mountainous terrain, banking system, and commitment to neutrality, Switzerland was seemingly secure in its peaceful stance. However, behind the scenes, Adolf Hitler harbored different plans. Despite public assurances, Hitler ordered a secret operation to invade Switzerland and Liechtenstein, known as Operation Tannenbaum.

Throughout the early years of World War II, Switzerland worked diligently to maintain its neutral status. This neutrality was crucial not only for the safety of its citizens but also for its role as a financial hub in Europe. Hitler, on several occasions, publicly assured the Swiss government that their neutrality would be respected. These assurances were a strategic ploy to keep Switzerland complacent and prevent them from aligning with the Allies or bolstering their defenses excessively.

Despite these assurances, Hitler ordered the Wehrmacht to draft a detailed plan for the invasion of Switzerland. This plan, known as Operation Tannenbaum (Operation Christmas Tree), was designed to bring Switzerland under German control and eliminate what Hitler disdainfully referred to as a "pimple on the face of Europe." The operation called for a two-pronged invasion, one attacking from the north through Germany and the other from the west through occupied France.

Switzerland's strategic importance cannot be overstated. Its mountainous terrain provided a natural fortress that could serve as a defensive stronghold. Additionally, Switzerland's banking system held significant financial assets that were of great interest to the Nazis. Controlling Switzerland would have provided Hitler with not only a strategic military advantage but also substantial economic resources to fuel his war machine.

Although Switzerland was neutral, it was far from defenseless. The Swiss military had developed extensive plans to defend the country in case of an invasion. Known as the National Redoubt, these plans involved utilizing the mountainous terrain to create a series of fortified positions that would be difficult for any invading force to capture. The Swiss also maintained a policy of universal conscription, ensuring that a significant portion of the population was trained and ready to defend the nation.

Liechtenstein, a tiny principality nestled between Switzerland and Austria, was also included in Operation Tannenbaum. Despite its small size, Liechtenstein's strategic location made it a target for Hitler's ambitions. The plan for Liechtenstein was similar to that for Switzerland: a swift and decisive invasion to bring the principality under Nazi control. Like Switzerland, Liechtenstein relied on its neutrality for protection and was ill-prepared for an invasion.

While Operation Tannenbaum was meticulously planned, several factors prevented its execution. The challenging terrain of the Alps would have posed significant logistical difficulties for the invading German forces. Additionally, the Swiss were well aware of the potential threat and had prepared their defenses accordingly. Moreover, the shifting priorities and the opening of multiple fronts stretched Germany's military resources thin, making an invasion of Switzerland less feasible.

Switzerland's Defiance

Throughout the war, Switzerland maintained a stance of cautious defiance. The Swiss government was well aware of the threat posed by Nazi Germany and took measures to bolster its defenses while also engaging in diplomatic efforts to dissuade an invasion. The presence of fortified positions and a well-trained militia served as a deterrent, convincing the Nazis that an invasion would be more trouble than it was worth.

Operation Tannenbaum remained one of Hitler's many unexecuted plans, hidden from the public eye until after the war. The discovery of these plans highlighted the precarious position Switzerland had been in throughout the conflict. Despite their official neutrality, the Swiss had been living under the shadow of potential invasion, prepared to defend their sovereignty at a moment's notice.

The revelation of Operation Tannenbaum after the war served as a reminder of the constant danger that neutral countries faced during World War II. It underscored the extent of Hitler's ambitions and the ruthless lengths he was willing to go to achieve them. Today, the story of Operation Tannenbaum stands as a testament to Switzerland's resilience and the ever-present threat of tyranny during one of the darkest periods in history.

- Beyond strategic and military considerations, Hitler was also interested in Switzerland's vast financial resources. Swiss banks held significant amounts of gold and other assets, much of it belonging to Nazi Germany, and gaining control over these assets was a major incentive for the invasion plan.
- Throughout the war, Switzerland became a hub of espionage and intelligence activities. Both the Allies and Axis powers had spies operating within Swiss borders, and the country played a critical role in the exchange of information. The high level of intelligence activity in Switzerland made it a point of interest for the Nazis.
- Despite its neutrality, the Swiss Air Force had several skirmishes with German aircraft during the war. Swiss fighters intercepted and, in some cases, shot down German planes that violated Swiss airspace, showcasing Switzerland's readiness to defend its sovereignty even in the skies.

Operation Unthinkable: Churchill's Secret War Plan

In the final days of World War II, as the Allies celebrated their hard-won victory over Nazi Germany, a shadow of mistrust loomed over the future of Europe. Winston Churchill, the indomitable British Prime Minister, foresaw potential conflicts with the Soviet Union, despite their wartime alliance. In a move that remained classified for over fifty years, Churchill ordered the creation of 'Operation Unthinkable,' a plan that contemplated a surprise attack on Soviet forces stationed in Germany.

In May 1945, with Germany defeated and Europe in ruins, the Allied powers turned their attention to the post-war order. However, tensions were already surfacing between the Western Allies and the Soviet Union. Churchill, wary of Soviet intentions and their increasing control over Eastern Europe, sought to prepare for a possible future conflict. He commissioned his military chiefs to develop a plan that would address the growing threat posed by the Soviet Union.

The Plan's Objectives

Operation Unthinkable consisted of two primary scenarios: a defensive operation to secure Western Europe in case of Soviet aggression, and a more audacious plan for a preemptive strike against Soviet forces. The offensive plan envisioned a surprise attack on Soviet positions in Germany to force the USSR to negotiate from a position of weakness. The objective was to ensure the security and independence of Western European nations and to prevent Soviet domination of the continent.

Churchill's planners faced several daunting challenges. The Red Army, battle-hardened and numerically superior, occupied vast swathes of Europe. A direct confrontation would require substantial manpower and resources, which were already strained after years of relentless conflict. The British military, along with American and Allied forces, would have to rely on a swift and decisive strike to achieve any measure of success.

Upon reviewing the feasibility of Operation Unthinkable, military strategists concluded that the plan was fraught with risks. The likelihood of success was slim given the Soviet numerical advantage and the potential for prolonged and devastating warfare. The logistical complexities of launching such an operation, coupled with the uncertain political ramifications, made the plan highly contentious. Ultimately, the plan was deemed too perilous to pursue.

Secrecy and Sensitivity

The existence of Operation Unthinkable was kept a closely guarded secret. Churchill understood the delicate nature of the proposal and the potential diplomatic fallout should it be revealed. Relations with the Soviet Union were already tenuous, and any hint of an aggressive strategy could exacerbate tensions and derail the fragile post-war peace. Consequently, the plan was classified and shelved, remaining undisclosed for decades.

It wasn't until 1998, more than fifty years after the end of World War II, that the details of Operation Unthinkable were finally declassified. The British government, in an effort to provide a more comprehensive historical account of the war and its aftermath, released the documents related to the plan. The revelation of Churchill's secret plan surprised many and sparked debates about the early origins of the Cold War.

The declassification of Operation Unthinkable offered valuable insights into the post-war geopolitical landscape and the strategic thinking of Allied leaders. It underscored the profound mistrust that existed between the Western Allies and the Soviet Union even before the war had fully concluded. The plan also highlighted Churchill's foresight in recognizing the potential for future conflicts in Europe and his determination to safeguard Western interests.

Winston Churchill's legacy as a wartime leader is well established, but Operation Unthinkable adds a complex dimension to his historical image. It reveals his pragmatic approach to international relations and his willingness to consider extreme measures to protect British and Allied interests. While the plan was never executed, it remains a testament to the precarious balance of power in the immediate aftermath of World War II.

Operation Unthinkable stands as a fascinating and sobering reminder of the turbulent early days of the post-war era. Churchill's secret plan to confront the Soviet Union, kept hidden for over half a century, reflects the deep-seated anxieties and strategic dilemmas faced by the Allied leaders. The eventual declassification of the plan provides a fuller understanding of the complexities and challenges of maintaining peace in a world emerging from the shadows of global conflict.

1. British-American Cooperation

- The plan relied heavily on the cooperation of American forces. Churchill believed that a successful offensive against the Soviets would require significant support from the United States, underscoring the importance of the Anglo-American alliance.

2. Contingency Planning

- Operation Unthinkable was one of the first major contingency plans of the Cold War era. It set a precedent for future military strategies and alliances aimed at countering Soviet influence, including the formation of NATO in 1949.

3. Stalin's Awareness

- Although the plan remained secret for decades, there were indications that Soviet leader Joseph Stalin was aware of Western concerns and potential plans for conflict. This awareness likely contributed to the Soviet Union's own preparations and strategies during the early Cold War period.

Who Am I – Hard

1. I was a German field marshal known for my leadership in North Africa. Nicknamed the "Desert Fox," I gained fame for my tactical brilliance and was later involved in a plot to overthrow Hitler.
   Who am I?

2. I was a Soviet female sniper during World War II, credited with 309 confirmed kills. My prowess earned me the nickname "Lady Death," and I became a celebrated war hero.
   Who am I?

3. I was an Australian general who played a key role in the Pacific Theater, particularly in the defense of New Guinea and the subsequent Allied counteroffensives.
   Who am I?

4. I was a French general who played a significant role in the liberation of Paris. Later, I served as the first commander of NATO's Allied Land Forces Central Europe.
   Who am I?

5. I was a Finnish sniper credited with over 500 confirmed kills, making me one of the deadliest snipers in history. My effectiveness in the Winter War earned me the nickname "White Death."
   Who am I?

Answers

1. **Erwin Rommel**, born in 1891 in Heidenheim, Germany, was a German field marshal known for his leadership in North Africa during World War II. Nicknamed the "Desert Fox," Rommel gained fame for his tactical brilliance in the North African Campaign. Despite his loyalty to Germany, he was implicated in the July 20 plot to overthrow Hitler and was forced to commit suicide in 1944. Rommel is remembered as one of Germany's most respected military leaders.

2. **Lyudmila Pavlichenko**, born in 1916 in Bila Tserkva, Ukraine, was a Soviet sniper during World War II, credited with 309 confirmed kills. Her extraordinary marksmanship earned her the nickname "Lady Death." She became a celebrated war hero and was invited to tour the United States and Canada to advocate for the Soviet war effort. Pavlichenko's legacy remains as one of the most effective and celebrated female snipers in history.

3. **Thomas Blamey**, born in 1884 in Wagga Wagga, Australia, was an Australian general who played a key role in the Pacific Theater during World War II. He was instrumental in the defense of New Guinea and led the Allied counteroffensives that pushed Japanese forces out of the region. Blamey was the only Australian to attain the rank of Field Marshal and is remembered for his significant contributions to the Allied war effort in the Pacific.

4. **Jacques Massu**, born in 1908 in Châlons-sur-Marne, France, was a French general who played a significant role in the liberation of Paris during World War II. He later served as the first commander of NATO's Allied Land Forces Central Europe. Massu's leadership in both World War II and post-war military organizations made him a prominent figure in French and NATO military history.

5. **Simo Häyhä**, born in 1905 in Rautjärvi, Finland, was a Finnish sniper credited with over 500 confirmed kills during the Winter War against the Soviet Union. His effectiveness in the harsh winter conditions earned him the nickname "White Death." Häyhä's remarkable skills and resilience made him one of the deadliest snipers in history, and he remains a legendary figure in military history.

Mad Jack Churchill: The Bagpipe-Playing, Sword-Wielding Soldier

You're in the heat of World War II, bullets whizzing past, explosions rocking the ground, and in the middle of it all, a man strides confidently with a broadsword in hand and bagpipes under his arm. No, this isn't a scene from a Monty Python sketch; this is the real-life legend of John Malcolm Thorpe Fleming Churchill, affectionately known as "Mad Jack." With a penchant for medieval weaponry and a flair for the dramatic, Mad Jack was the kind of character that history teachers dream about when trying to make their classes interesting.

Born in Surrey, England, in 1906, Jack Churchill had adventure in his blood from day one. After graduating from the Royal Military College at Sandhurst, he joined the Manchester Regiment and soon found himself stationed in Burma. It was here that he began to stand out—not for his military maneuvers, but for his uncanny ability to make heads turn by practicing the longbow and playing the bagpipes. His colleagues might have thought he was a bit eccentric, but little did they know, Mad Jack was just warming up.

Fast forward to 1940 and the chaos of Dunkirk. While most soldiers were focused on evacuating, Mad Jack took a more...medieval approach. Armed with his trusty longbow and broadsword, he took down a German soldier, reportedly becoming the last person in modern warfare to kill with a longbow. Imagine the look on that soldier's face—probably thinking he'd been transported back to the Hundred Years' War!

Then there was the raid on the Norwegian town of Vågsøy in 1941. As the landing craft hit the shore, Mad Jack jumped out, playing "March of the Cameron Men" on his bagpipes. He then threw a grenade, unsheathed his broadsword, and charged into battle. Now, if you're the enemy and you see a guy coming at you like he's auditioning for "Braveheart 2," you're probably going to reconsider your life choices. His audacious antics not only rallied his men but also left the enemy utterly bewildered.

Mad Jack's escapades didn't stop there. During the Italian campaign, he led a nighttime raid that resulted in the capture of 42 German soldiers—armed only with his broadsword and a few men. When he finally got captured in 1944, the Germans were likely scratching their heads, wondering if they had accidentally wandered into a historical reenactment. Sent to Sachsenhausen concentration camp, Jack, being the unstoppable force he was, managed to escape not once, but twice, walking 150 miles to Allied lines on his second attempt. Talk about determination!

Outside the battlefield, Mad Jack was no less colorful. He was a championship archer and even represented Britain at the World Archery Championships in Oslo in 1939. And let's not forget his bagpipes, which he played with as much passion as he fought with his sword. After the war, he continued to defy norms by becoming a professional surfer in Australia, riding waves long before it was cool.

Mad Jack's life was a patchwork of jaw-dropping feats and whimsical endeavors. He appeared in films like "Ivanhoe" and "A Yank at Oxford," proving that his talents were as varied as his weaponry. Despite his larger-than-life persona, he remained humble, often attributing his success to luck and the camaraderie of his fellow soldiers. His sense of humor and love for life made him a beloved figure among his peers, who fondly remembered his ability to bring a smile even in the darkest of times.

He passed away in 1996 at the age of 89, leaving behind a legacy that reads more like an adventure novel than a biography. Mad Jack Churchill's story is a vivid reminder that sometimes, the most extraordinary heroes are those who dare to be different, who face danger with a wink and a smile, and who remind us that life, even at its most perilous, is meant to be lived boldly.

So, the next time you find yourself in a tough spot, just think of Mad Jack, charging into battle with his sword raised high and his bagpipes blaring.

Timeline of WW2

World War II, one of the most significant and devastating conflicts in history, spanned from 1939 to 1945, involving major global powers divided into the Allies and the Axis. The war reshaped the world's political landscape, leading to the emergence of the United States and the Soviet Union as superpowers and setting the stage for the Cold War.

The origins of World War II can be traced back to the aftermath of World War I and the Treaty of Versailles, which imposed harsh penalties on Germany. Economic turmoil and nationalistic fervor facilitated the rise of totalitarian regimes, notably Adolf Hitler's Nazi Germany and Benito Mussolini's Fascist Italy. Hitler's aggressive expansionist policies, including the remilitarization of the Rhineland, the annexation of Austria (Anschluss), and the invasion of Czechoslovakia, heightened tensions in Europe.

1939

- **September 1:** Germany invades Poland using blitzkrieg tactics, a rapid and intense military campaign, prompting Britain and France to declare war on Germany on September 3. This invasion marks the official start of World War II. The swift German advance quickly overwhelms Polish forces, and by late September, Poland is divided between Nazi Germany and the Soviet Union, following the secret terms of the Molotov-Ribbentrop Pact.
- **September 17:** The Soviet Union invades eastern Poland, aligning with Nazi Germany as per their secret agreement, effectively carving Poland into German and Soviet territories. This invasion ensures that Poland is quickly subdued, preventing a prolonged conflict on Germany's eastern front.

1940

- **April-June:** Germany invades Denmark and Norway on April 9, securing critical access to the North Sea and valuable natural resources, particularly Swedish iron ore transported through Norway.
- This swift campaign results in the resignation of British Prime Minister Neville Chamberlain, who is replaced by Winston Churchill on May 10, a leader more determined to confront Nazi aggression. The subsequent invasions of Belgium, the Netherlands, and France see rapid German advances, leading to the fall of France in June and the establishment of the Vichy regime.
- **June 10:** Italy declares war on Britain and France, joining the Axis powers and opening new fronts in North Africa and the Mediterranean, further complicating the Allies' strategic situation.
- **July-October:** The Battle of Britain ensues as Germany attempts to gain air superiority over Britain in preparation for a planned invasion (Operation Sea Lion). The Royal Air Force (RAF) successfully defends against the Luftwaffe's sustained bombing campaign, marking Germany's first significant defeat and demonstrating that air power can decisively impact the outcome of wars.

1941

- **June 22:** Operation Barbarossa, Germany's massive invasion of the Soviet Union, begins, marking the largest military operation in history. Despite initial successes, the German advance stalls due to logistical challenges and the onset of the harsh Russian winter, leading to prolonged and brutal combat on the Eastern Front.
- **December 7:** Japan attacks Pearl Harbor, devastating the U.S. Pacific Fleet and leading to the United States' formal

entry into World War II on December 8. This surprise attack galvanizes American public opinion and marks a significant shift in the war's dynamics, as the U.S. mobilizes its vast industrial and military resources against the Axis powers.

1942

- **June 4-7:** The Battle of Midway occurs, with U.S. forces achieving a decisive victory by sinking four Japanese aircraft carriers. This battle is a turning point in the Pacific Theater, halting Japanese expansion and shifting the strategic initiative to the Allies.
- **August-November:** The Battle of Stalingrad begins, resulting in a crucial Soviet victory after months of grueling urban warfare. This battle significantly weakens German forces and marks the beginning of a major Soviet offensive pushing westward.

1943

- **July 9-August 17:** The Allied invasion of Sicily, codenamed Operation Husky, successfully leads to the toppling of Mussolini's regime and Italy's subsequent surrender on September 3. However, German forces continue to resist, turning Italy into a prolonged battleground.

1944

- **June 6:** D-Day, the Allied invasion of Normandy, establishes a crucial second front in Western Europe. This massive amphibious assault involves extensive coordination and leads to the liberation of France and the eventual push towards Germany.
- **December 16:** The Battle of the Bulge, Germany's last major offensive in the West, begins. Despite initial gains, the

offensive is ultimately repelled by Allied forces, depleting Germany's reserves and hastening the end of the war in Europe.

1945

- **April 30:** Adolf Hitler commits suicide in his Berlin bunker as Soviet forces encircle the city, signaling the imminent collapse of Nazi Germany.
- **May 8:** V-E Day (Victory in Europe Day) is celebrated as Germany surrenders unconditionally to the Allies, ending the war in Europe and leading to the occupation and division of Germany.
- **August 6 and 9:** The United States drops atomic bombs on Hiroshima and Nagasaki, resulting in unprecedented destruction and leading to Japan's surrender. These bombings demonstrate the devastating power of nuclear weapons and underscore the Allies' determination to end the war swiftly.
- **September 2:** V-J Day (Victory over Japan Day) marks Japan's formal surrender aboard the USS Missouri, bringing World War II to an official end and beginning the process of post-war.

Cult of Hitler

Early Life and Ideology Formation

Adolf Hitler was born on April 20, 1889, in Braunau am Inn, a small town in Austria-Hungary. His early years were marked by a troubled family life and academic underachievement. After the death of his parents, Hitler moved to Vienna, where he struggled as an artist and developed his early political views. During this period, he became increasingly exposed to nationalist and anti-Semitic ideologies, which were prevalent in Vienna at the time. These ideas profoundly influenced his worldview, laying the groundwork for his later political agenda.

Mein Kampf and Ideological Blueprint

After serving in World War I, where he was decorated for bravery but remained a low-ranking soldier, Hitler joined the German Workers' Party (DAP) in 1919, which was later renamed the National Socialist German Workers' Party (NSDAP or Nazi Party). In 1923, Hitler attempted to seize power in the failed Beer Hall Putsch in Munich, for which he was imprisoned. During his incarceration, he authored "Mein Kampf" ("My Struggle"), a two-volume work published in 1925 and 1926. This book outlined his ideology, including his virulent anti-Semitism, belief in Aryan racial superiority, and the need for Lebensraum (living space) for the German people. "Mein Kampf" served as a manifesto for the Nazi movement, articulating Hitler's vision for Germany's future and his plan to overturn the Treaty of Versailles.

Rise to Power

Following his release from prison, Hitler focused on rebuilding the Nazi Party, transforming it into a significant political force through charismatic oratory and relentless propaganda. The economic turmoil of the Great Depression in the late 1920s and early 1930s created fertile ground for his message, as many Germans were disillusioned with the Weimar Republic's handling of the crisis. The Nazis capitalized on widespread economic hardship, fear of communism, and nationalist resentment.

In the 1932 elections, the Nazi Party became the largest party in the Reichstag, Germany's parliament, though they did not achieve an outright majority. Despite initial reluctance, President Paul von Hindenburg appointed Hitler as Chancellor of Germany on January 30, 1933, believing he could be controlled and used to stabilize the government. However, Hitler quickly consolidated power through a combination of political maneuvering and intimidation.

The Cult of Hitler

Once in power, Hitler established a totalitarian regime characterized by the "Führerprinzip" (leader principle), where he was the ultimate authority. The Reichstag Fire in February 1933 provided a pretext to push through the Reichstag Fire Decree, which suspended civil liberties and allowed for the arrest of political opponents. The Enabling Act, passed in March 1933, gave Hitler dictatorial powers by allowing him to enact laws without parliamentary consent.

Hitler's regime skillfully used propaganda to cultivate a cult of personality around him, portraying him as Germany's savior. The Nazi propaganda machine, led by Joseph Goebbels, glorified Hitler through speeches, rallies, films, and the press, fostering a sense of unity and unquestioning loyalty to the Führer. The regime's repressive measures, combined with economic recovery programs, solidified Hitler's grip on power, leading to the aggressive expansionist policies that would plunge the world into World War II.

- Before entering politics, Hitler aspired to be an artist and twice applied to the Academy of Fine Arts Vienna but was rejected both times.
- Hitler adopted a vegetarian diet in the early 1930s, partly due to his chronic digestive issues and his strong aversion to animal cruelty.
- During World War II, Hitler was regularly injected with methamphetamine by his personal physician, Dr. Theodor Morell, which may have influenced his erratic behavior and decision-making.
- Hitler survived over 40 assassination attempts, the most famous being the July 20, 1944, plot involving a bomb planted by Colonel Claus von Stauffenberg.
- Despite the party culture surrounding him, Hitler abstained from alcohol, promoting a public image of discipline and purity.
- Hitler was very fond of his German Shepherds, particularly a dog named Blondi, which he had with him until his death.
- There is a popular, though unverified, myth that Hitler had only one testicle, allegedly lost during World War I.
- Hitler was a great admirer of composer Richard Wagner, whose operas inspired his vision of German nationalism and Aryan superiority.
- As a child, Hitler aspired to become a priest and even sang in the choir of a monastery.
- Hitler was awarded the Iron Cross, First Class, for bravery during World War I, an honor not commonly given to corporals.
- Hitler and several high-ranking Nazis were fascinated by the occult and mystical theories, influencing some of their ideological beliefs.

- Hitler was obsessed with physical fitness and promoted sports and exercise as essential components of Aryan strength.
- Hitler meticulously rehearsed his speeches, practicing in front of a mirror to perfect his gestures and expressions.
- Hitler had grand architectural plans for Berlin, intending to transform it into "Welthauptstadt Germania," a world capital of colossal proportions. Despite possessing chemical weapons,
- Hitler refrained from using them on the battlefield, possibly due to his own traumatic experiences with gas attacks in World War I. Hitler committed suicide on April 30, 1945, in his Berlin bunker alongside Eva Braun, whom he had married just hours before their deaths.

"If you win, you need not have to explain...If you lose, you should not be there to explain!" — Adolf Hitler

Benito Mussolini's Life Through His Quotes

"It is better to live one day as a lion than 100 years as a sheep."

This quote reflects Mussolini's belief in bold action and the glorification of strength and power. Born on July 29, 1883, in Predappio, Italy, Benito Mussolini's early life was marked by his involvement in socialist politics and journalism. He founded the Fascist Party in 1919, advocating for a strong, centralized government and nationalist policies, setting the stage for his eventual rise to power as Italy's dictator.

"The truth is that men are tired of liberty."

Mussolini's view on authoritarianism is encapsulated in this quote. He believed that the chaos and inefficiencies of democracy could only be resolved through a dictatorial regime. After becoming Prime Minister in 1922, Mussolini gradually dismantled democratic institutions in Italy, establishing a totalitarian state where dissent was not tolerated, and individual freedoms were severely restricted.

"Fascism is a religion. The twentieth century will be known in history as the century of Fascism."

This quote reflects Mussolini's vision of Fascism as not just a political system but a comprehensive ideology. He sought to create a new societal order based on the principles of Fascism, emphasizing nationalism, militarism, and the subjugation of individual interests to the needs of the state. Mussolini's regime aimed to transform Italian society through propaganda, education, and strict control over all aspects of life.

"Democracy is beautiful in theory; in practice, it is a fallacy."

Mussolini's skepticism about democracy is evident in this quote. He viewed democratic processes as weak and inefficient, believing that only a strong, centralized authority could effectively govern. This belief underpinned his efforts to establish a dictatorship, where power was concentrated in his hands, and opposition was ruthlessly suppressed.

"War is to man what maternity is to a woman."

This quote underscores Mussolini's glorification of war and conflict as essential aspects of human existence and national strength. Under his leadership, Italy pursued aggressive foreign policies, including the invasion of Ethiopia in 1935 and participation in World War II alongside Nazi Germany. Mussolini's militaristic ambitions ultimately led to significant losses and suffering for Italy.

"The function of a citizen and a soldier are inseparable."

Mussolini believed in the militarization of society, where every citizen had a duty to serve the state, both in civil life and in military endeavors. His regime promoted the idea of a militarized state where discipline, loyalty, and service were paramount. This ideology was reflected in the extensive use of military parades, youth organizations, and propaganda to instill these values in the Italian population.

"Better to break than to bend."

Mussolini's defiance and determination are evident in this quote. He consistently portrayed himself as a strong and uncompromising leader, unwilling to yield to opposition or external pressures. This attitude contributed to his initial popularity but also to his downfall, as his inflexible policies and alliances led Italy into disastrous conflicts and ultimately his own capture and execution.

"The press of Italy is free, freer than the press of any other country, so long as it supports the regime."

This quote highlights Mussolini's approach to media and propaganda. While claiming to support freedom of the press, in reality, Mussolini's regime exercised strict control over the media, using it as a tool to disseminate Fascist ideology and suppress dissent. Independent journalism was effectively eradicated, and the state-controlled narrative dominated Italian public life.

"Socialism is a fraud, a comedy, a phantom, a blackmail."

Mussolini's disillusionment with socialism is reflected in this quote. Although he began his political career as a socialist, he later rejected socialism in favor of nationalism and Fascism. His shift in ideology was driven by his belief that socialism was incapable of addressing the needs of the nation and that only a strong, authoritarian state could achieve greatness.

> *"Let us have a dagger between our teeth, a bomb in our hands, and an infinite scorn in our hearts."*

This quote epitomizes Mussolini's aggressive and violent rhetoric. He encouraged the use of violence and intimidation to achieve political goals and maintain control. The Fascist Blackshirts, paramilitary groups loyal to Mussolini, employed these tactics to suppress opposition and enforce the regime's policies, contributing to the climate of fear and repression in Fascist Italy.

Did you know?

Before rising to power, Benito Mussolini worked as a schoolteacher and a journalist. His background in journalism helped him master the art of propaganda, which he used effectively to build his political movement and control public opinion. Mussolini's ability to manipulate media and public perception was a key factor in his consolidation of power and the establishment of his totalitarian regime.

The Death of Mussolini: The Downfall of Italian Fascism

Benito Mussolini rose to power in Italy by capitalizing on social unrest and economic instability after World War I. He established the Fascist Party in 1919, promoting a platform of nationalism, militarism, and anti-communism. In 1922, Mussolini and his Blackshirts marched on Rome, and he was appointed Prime Minister. Over the next few years, he dismantled democratic institutions, established a totalitarian regime, and embarked on aggressive expansionist policies.

However, Mussolini's alliance with Nazi Germany and his involvement in World War II proved disastrous for Italy. The Italian military suffered numerous defeats, and the country was soon occupied by Allied forces. By 1943, Mussolini's grip on power was slipping. King Victor Emmanuel III had him arrested, and a new government signed an armistice with the Allies.

Despite his arrest, German forces rescued Mussolini and installed him as the head of the Italian Social Republic, a puppet state in Northern Italy. As the war turned further against the Axis powers, Mussolini's control weakened. By April 1945, Allied and partisan forces were closing in. Realizing the imminent collapse of his regime, Mussolini attempted to flee to Switzerland with his mistress, Clara Petacci, and a small entourage.

On April 27, 1945, Mussolini was captured by Italian partisans near the village of Dongo on Lake Como. The next day, he and Petacci were executed by firing squad. Their bodies were then taken to Milan, where they were publicly displayed in Piazzale Loreto. Mussolini's body, along with those of other executed

Fascists, was hung upside down from a metal girder at a petrol station, subjected to public scorn and abuse.

After the public display, Mussolini's body was buried in an unmarked grave in the Musocco cemetery in Milan. However, this was not the end of the story. In 1946, Mussolini's body was stolen by Fascist supporters, but it was recovered by the authorities a few months later. His remains were then kept in a series of secret locations to prevent further attempts at exhumation.

Finally, in 1957, Mussolini's body was returned to his family and buried in the family crypt in Predappio, his birthplace. Predappio has since become a site of pilgrimage for neo-Fascists and those who still admire Mussolini's legacy, despite the widespread condemnation of his regime's actions.

The Fate of Mussolini's Brain

In a bizarre twist, parts of Mussolini's brain were sent to the United States for examination by American scientists. This examination aimed to determine whether there were any pathological conditions that could explain his behavior and leadership style. However, the findings were inconclusive. In 1966, the brain fragments were returned to Mussolini's widow, Rachele.

Mussolini's death marked the definitive end of Fascism in Italy. His regime, characterized by its violent repression, aggressive nationalism, and disastrous wartime alliances, left a lasting scar on Italian history. The public desecration of his body symbolized the utter rejection of his ideology by the Italian people.

Yet, the legacy of Mussolini and Fascism remains controversial. While most view him as a tyrant whose policies brought ruin to Italy, a small minority continues to see him as a strong leader who brought order and national pride. This dichotomy is evident in the annual gatherings in Predappio and the ongoing debates about Fascism's place in Italian history.

Did you know?

Mussolini's death and the macabre display of his body have been depicted in various films and books, illustrating the dramatic end of one of history's most notorious dictators. His life and death serve as a stark reminder of the perils of totalitarianism and the destructive consequences of unchecked power.

Best World War II Films

1. Saving Private Ryan (1998)

- **Realistic Portrayal:** The opening 27-minute D-Day sequence is known for its brutal realism, with veterans stating it closely resembles the actual events.
- **Veteran Reactions:** Many WWII veterans were unable to watch the film due to its intense and realistic depiction of war.
- **Director's Dedication:** Steven Spielberg used actual amputees to portray soldiers who lost limbs in the combat scenes to enhance authenticity.

2. Schindler's List (1993)

- **True Story:** The film is based on the true story of Oskar Schindler, a German businessman who saved over 1,000 Jews during the Holocaust.
- **Emotional Impact:** During filming, Spielberg had to take breaks due to the emotional toll of directing the harrowing scenes.
- **Black-and-White Symbolism:** The film is shot in black-and-white, except for the little girl in the red coat, symbolizing innocence amidst horror.

3. Dunkirk (2017)

- **Chronological Complexity:** The film uses three different timelines to tell the story of the Dunkirk evacuation from land, sea, and air perspectives.
- **Minimal CGI:** Director Christopher Nolan used minimal CGI, opting for practical effects and real ships and planes to recreate the events.

- **Tension Building:** The score by Hans Zimmer uses a ticking clock sound throughout the film to create a sense of relentless tension.

4. The Pianist (2002)

- **Based on Memoir:** The film is based on the autobiography of Władysław Szpilman, a Polish-Jewish pianist who survived the Holocaust.
- **Starvation Diet:** Actor Adrien Brody lost 30 pounds and learned to play the piano to authentically portray Szpilman.
- **Real Locations:** Many scenes were filmed in actual locations in Warsaw, adding to the film's historical accuracy.

5. Inglourious Basterds (2009)

- **Alternate History:** The film presents an alternate history where a group of Jewish soldiers plot to assassinate Nazi leaders, diverging from actual events.
- **Multilingual Dialogue:** Quentin Tarantino insisted on characters speaking their native languages, resulting in English, German, French, and Italian dialogue.
- **Bizarre Ending:** The film ends with a fictionalized and explosive assassination of Hitler, deviating wildly from historical facts.

6. The Thin Red Line (1998)

- **Philosophical Approach:** The film is known for its philosophical and poetic approach to the war, focusing on the internal struggles of soldiers.
- **Ensemble Cast:** Features an ensemble cast, with many big-name actors having only a few minutes of screen time.
- **Real Soldiers:** Several actual World War II veterans appeared in the film, providing authenticity to the portrayal of combat.

7. Letters from Iwo Jima (2006)

- **Japanese Perspective:** Directed by Clint Eastwood, the film tells the story of the Battle of Iwo Jima from the Japanese perspective.
- **Companion Piece:** It is a companion film to "Flags of Our Fathers," which depicts the American perspective of the same battle.
- **Historical Letters:** The film was inspired by actual letters written by Japanese soldiers during the battle, providing an intimate look at their experiences.

8. The Great Escape (1963)

- **True Story:** Based on the true story of the mass escape of Allied prisoners from Stalag Luft III, a German POW camp.
- **Iconic Motorcycle Chase:** The famous motorcycle chase scene, performed by Steve McQueen, was almost entirely performed by the actor himself.
- **Real-Life Connections:** Several of the actors, including Donald Pleasence, had real-life experiences as prisoners of war during World War II.

9. Patton (1970)

- **Epic Performance:** George C. Scott's portrayal of General George S. Patton is widely regarded as one of the greatest performances in film history.
- **Controversial Figure:** The film explores the complex and controversial nature of Patton, highlighting both his brilliance and flaws.
- **Opening Monologue:** The film opens with a famous monologue in front of a giant American flag, which has become an iconic scene in cinema.

10. A Bridge Too Far (1977)

- **All-Star Cast:** Features an all-star cast including Sean Connery, Michael Caine, and Robert Redford, among others.
- **True Events:** The film depicts the failed Operation Market Garden, an ambitious Allied operation to capture key bridges in the Netherlands.
- **Authentic Equipment:** Used actual World War II military equipment and vehicles, including tanks and planes, to recreate the battle scenes accurately.

Did You Know?

- "Saving Private Ryan" realism caused such intense reactions that some theaters provided counseling for veterans after screenings.
- In "Schindler's List," director Steven Spielberg took no salary, considering it "blood money" and instead donated his earnings to the Shoah Foundation.
- The ticking clock sound in "Dunkirk" was created using director Christopher Nolan's own pocket watch, enhancing the film's authenticity and tension.
- Adrien Brody, who portrayed Szpilman in "The Pianist," sold all his belongings and moved to Europe to experience the pianist's displacement and loss.
- "Inglourious Basterds" used genuine World War II weaponry and uniforms to enhance the film's authenticity, despite its fictional storyline.

Propaganda

Allied Enlistment

Propaganda played a crucial role in motivating enlistment on the Allied side during World War II. Governments utilized powerful imagery, emotive slogans, and compelling narratives to galvanize public support and encourage men to join the military. Posters depicted heroic soldiers and sailors, often accompanied by messages that appealed to patriotism, duty, and the defense of freedom and democracy. Campaigns such as "Uncle Sam Wants You" in the United States and similar efforts in the United Kingdom and Commonwealth nations emphasized the moral imperative to fight against tyranny and protect the homeland. These messages were designed to instill a sense of urgency and responsibility, portraying enlistment as a noble and necessary act. Additionally, propaganda highlighted the atrocities committed by Axis powers, framing the conflict as a clear struggle between good and evil, which further motivated individuals to enlist. The widespread dissemination of such propaganda through newspapers, radio broadcasts, and public posters significantly influenced public opinion and increased recruitment numbers.

Axis Enlistment

On the Axis side, propaganda was equally influential in encouraging enlistment, though it often took on a different tone and focus. In Nazi Germany, propaganda under Joseph Goebbels' Ministry of Propaganda emphasized themes of nationalism, racial superiority, and the defense of the Fatherland. Posters and films glorified the German soldier as the defender of Aryan values and the bulwark against Bolshevism and Western decadence. Similarly, in Japan, propaganda stressed themes of loyalty to the Emperor, the purity of the Japanese race, and the divine destiny of Japan to lead Asia. Messages promoted the idea of self-sacrifice for the greater good of the nation, often romanticizing the notion of dying for one's country. The portrayal of enemies as subhuman or barbaric also played a significant role in motivating Japanese and German citizens to enlist, driven by a sense of duty to protect their nation from perceived existential threats. These propaganda efforts were disseminated through various media, including films, radio broadcasts.

Walt Disney's Role in War Support through Propaganda

Walt Disney played a significant role in generating support for the war effort during World War II by leveraging his animation studio's resources and creative talents to produce a wide range of propaganda films and educational content. Disney's studio created numerous short films, training videos, and propaganda pieces that were distributed to both military personnel and the general public. One of the most notable contributions was the creation of iconic characters like Donald Duck, who starred in several war-themed cartoons such as "Der Fuehrer's Face" (1943). This particular film, which satirized Nazi Germany and its leadership, won an Academy Award and became a powerful tool in boosting American morale and promoting the absurdity of the Axis powers. Additionally, Disney produced educational films like "Victory Through Air Power" (1943), which emphasized the importance of air supremacy and strategic bombing, thereby supporting the military's strategic objectives and fostering public understanding of key war strategies.

Educational and Training Contributions

Beyond entertainment, Disney's studio significantly contributed to the war effort by producing over 400,000 feet of educational film, totaling around 68 hours of continuous film, designed to educate and train military personnel. These films covered a wide range of topics, including navigation, aircraft identification, and the proper use of military equipment. One notable series was the "Why We Fight" series, which aimed to educate soldiers and the public about the reasons behind America's involvement in the war and the broader context of the global conflict. Furthermore, Disney's studio created instructional films for the U.S. Navy, such as "The New Spirit" (1942), which encouraged Americans to pay their income taxes promptly to support the war effort financially. These films were instrumental in simplifying complex information, making it accessible and engaging for both military personnel and civilians. Through these diverse contributions, Walt Disney and his studio played a crucial role in bolstering public support for the war, enhancing military training, and promoting the Allied cause.

Churchill's Dilemma

During World War II, after the fall of France in 1940, Prime Minister Winston Churchill faced a critical and complex decision. With the French fleet at risk of falling into German hands, Churchill ordered an attack on the French naval fleet stationed at Mers-el-Kébir, Algeria. This preemptive strike aimed to prevent the powerful French ships from being used by the Axis powers, which could have significantly altered the naval balance in favor of Nazi Germany. Churchill's decision was driven by the urgent need to ensure that the French fleet would not augment the naval strength of the enemy. The British government offered the French multiple options to avoid conflict, including joining the British fleet, sailing to a neutral port, or scuttling the ships. When these options were refused, Churchill authorized the attack, resulting in the sinking of several French ships and significant loss of life. This controversial action underscored the harsh realities of wartime decision-making and the lengths to which Churchill was willing to go to safeguard Britain and its allies from potential threats.

- The attack on Mers-el-Kébir occurred on July 3, 1940, shortly after France signed an armistice with Germany.
- The British fleet was commanded by Admiral James Somerville during the Mers-el-Kébir operation.
- The French battleship Bretagne exploded during the attack, resulting in over 1,000 French sailors' deaths.
- Churchill described the decision as the most "hateful" of his life but deemed it necessary for Britain's survival.
- The operation was codenamed "Operation Catapult." The French fleet at Mers-el-Kébir included battleships, cruisers, and destroyers.
- The attack strained relations between Britain and Vichy France, leading to increased hostilities.
- Churchill's decision was supported by the War Cabinet but met with mixed reactions among the British public and officials.

Thank You!

Thank you for joining us on this incredible journey through some of the most fascinating and lesser-known stories of World War II. We hope you found these tales as captivating and eye-opening as we did. Your interest and curiosity help keep these important pieces of history alive.

For more information, additional stories, and exclusive content, please scan the QR code below. We also value your feedback and would love to hear your thoughts. If you enjoyed this book, please consider leaving a review on Amazon. Your reviews help us reach more readers and continue to share these amazing stories.

Printed in Great Britain
by Amazon